Contents

The author and his wo

Background t

The Shadow o

Plot and themes

Style 17

Characters 20

Act summaries and otes 26

The Plough and the Stars 37

Plot and themes 37

Style 39

Characters 41

Act summaries and textual notes 52

General revision questions 76

Page references in these Notes are to the Macmillan Papermac edition of *Three Plays by Sean O'Casey*, but as each play and act is analysed separately, the Notes can be used with other editions of the plays

To the student

A close reading of the plays is the student's primary task. These Notes will help to increase your understanding and appreciation of each play, and to stimulate *your own* thinking about it. *They are in no way intended as a substitute* for a thorough knowledge of the plays. You would find it helpful to attend a performance of one or both of the plays.

The author and his work

Sean O'Casey was born in Dublin on 30 March 1880. He was christened John, the family name being just 'Casey', but he converted this to 'O'Casey' shortly after the Abbey Theatre accepted his first play. He was the youngest of a family of thirteen, only five of whom survived infancy. His parents were Protestants; his father, a clerk, died at the age of forty-nine, leaving his wife to bring up the remaining five children as best she could.

The family lived in one of the poorest areas of Dublin, a city which then had an unbelievably high death rate, particularly among children. Inevitably John suffered from the degrading conditions in which he lived, and he contracted a disease of the eyes, which was so severe that for many years he was in a state of near-blindness. Despite this he contrived to read as much as he could, and worshipped the martyred Irish leader Parnell, who had been hounded from office because of his affair with Kitty O'Shea. O'Casey came under the influence of the great Socialist leader among the Dublin poor, Jim Larkin, whose motto was, 'An injury to one is the concern of all.'

The squalid conditions in which the young John lived have since been movingly and graphically described by him. After periods of clerical work O'Casey became a labourer, then began to write, his reading being largely in Shakespeare and the popular 19th-century Irish dramatist Dion Boucicault. O'Casey and his brother were fond of acting; he was himself to appear in a Boucicault play. From the age of fourteen onwards he read voraciously in English literature, learned Irish (which he later taught), and by 1913 was secretary to the Irish Citizen Army. Later he resigned from this post on a question of principle. His strong socialist views meant that he was a great supporter of those who were under constant attack from the bishops for their radical and progressive views.

In 1918 O'Casey published some songs, generally satirical in tone, and a dramatic piece called *The Sacrifice of Thomas Ashe*. He then wrote an account of the Citizen Army which he had served so loyally. This book contains passages of fervent emotional intensity, initiatory sparks struck out in passion by the future dramatist. His roots were in socialism rather than nationalism, and consequently he was not personally involved in the Easter Rising of 1916, the major expression of the nationalist ideal. It is clear that he regarded his own allegiance primarily to the oppressed and suffering among whom he lived, and that he became progressively disenchanted with political and military action.

His first play *The Frost in Flower* was turned down by the Abbey Theatre, as were the next two – though Lady Gregory, the wealthy, influential patron of the arts, sent him detailed comments on the third. His fourth play, however, *On the Run*, was accepted and its title became *Shadow of a Gunman* (1923). As his biographer David Krause has put it, 'He had created his own rich and dramatic idiom out of the common language he had heard spoken in the slums of Dublin.' The success of O'Casey's next play *Juno and the Paycock* (1924), for which he received £25, persuaded him to devote himself entirely, if precariously, to full-time writing.

O'Casey was now forty-four years old. In 1926 *The Plough and the Stars* was produced at the Abbey Theatre: its audiences rioted in protest against O'Casey's treatment of the Easter Rising. O'Casey had held up a mirror to his countrymen; and his treatment of religion, his presentation of sex, and his inverted attitudes towards patriotism all threatened to challenge the view the Irish held of themselves. (These riots echo those which took place at the same theatre in 1907, at the production of J. M. Synge's *Playboy of the Western World*.)

O'Casey did not feel at home in the Abbey Theatre circle (even with the support and friendship of Lady Gregory), though he had established himself as an outstanding dramatist of his time. In 1926 he was awarded the Hawthornden Prize for *Juno and the Paycock*, and he was fêted in London, where he became friendly with George Bernard Shaw. Like Joyce before him, O'Casey left Dublin for exile, though, like Joyce, he continued to carry Dublin – and Ireland – in his heart.

In 1927 O'Casey married Eileen Carey, who had appeared in the London production of *The Plough and the Stars*; she was some twenty years his junior. From London he sent his next play *The Silver Tassie* (1929) to Yeats, who promptly rejected this fine anti-war experimental drama, castigating O'Casey for the Irish Civil War scene. This led to an increasingly bitter exchange between the two men and the breach between them never healed, though the play was in fact later performed in Dublin. O'Casey's next play, *Within the Gates* (1933), reacted against the Great Depression that followed the Wall Street crash of 1929, the major cause of excessive unemployment throughout the world in the early 1930s.

Since his plays aroused such passionate controversy, O'Casey now found himself writing more for publication than for performance. His series of essays *The Flying Wasp* (1937) is a pungent attack on the contemporary theatre, which regarded Nöel Coward and the middle-class glitter he personified as radical. O'Casey's own radicalism sprang from sturdier roots, and he had no time for the civilized veneer of English life. In 1937 he wrote *The Star Turns Red*, a declaration of his Communist views and of his determined opposition to the insidious spread of Fascism. It waited until 1940 for its production at the Unity Theatre, London.

Strangely, in the 1940s and 1950s he wrote three comedies, though each had its sardonic side and reflected both his disillusion and his compelling, undying faith in mankind. Moreover, he produced over a period of fifteen years some six volumes of autobiography, each of which deals with particular phases of his life and belief, and his vehement reactions to events and people. He suffered intense personal grief over the death of his son in 1956; he died after a heart attack on 18 September 1964, still expressing his ecstasy and joy in the experience of living. His early plays, two of which are dealt with in this Study Aid, remain his major contribution to the theatre; their language is endowed with the life of reality: the speech rhythms of the Dublin slums that are at once comic and poetic – symbolic, indeed, in their effects.

Further reading

Sean, Eileen O'Casey; ed. J. C. Trewin (Macmillan)

Sean O'Casey, W. A. Armstrong (Writers and their Work Series, British Council)

Sean O'Casey: The Man and his Work, David Krause (MacGibbon and Kee)

Autobiography: Vols 1–6 (Pan Books)

Background to the plays

The action of *The Plough and the Stars* is set in Dublin in November 1915 and Easter week 1916. Before we consider the play, therefore, it is as well to look at the general situation in Ireland from 1914 onwards.

In that year the country was still united with Great Britain though Home Rule was due to take effect very shortly. There was a British Army presence, as there had been for some time, but the Army was not one of occupation. There were garrison towns and areas used for manoeuvres, but they were no more under occupation than, say, Aldershot or Salisbury in England. In addition there were regiments recruited in Ireland – the Dublin Fusiliers and the Connaught Rangers for example – as well as large numbers of Irish soldiers in other British regiments. Poverty is a great recruiting sergeant.

There were two main police forces: the unarmed Dublin Metropolitan Police, and the carbine-armed Royal Ulster Constabulary, with its distinctive dark green, almost black uniform. This force was stationed in barracks throughout the country; for fear of retaliation against his family, no man could be stationed in his own home county. This force was established to deal with any local uprising that might occur but its main occupation was the prevention of smuggling or illicit whisky distilling, together with the execution of the innumerable duties of a country police force. There had been armed insurrections, destruction of crops and property, and mutilation of animals – bitterly spontaneous reactions to poverty and the government's total misunderstanding of the attitude of the people. There were several secret societies and patriotic clubs – Peter Flynn in *The Plough and the Stars* belonged to the Irish National Volunteers – and there were many Orange lodges in the Northern counties. Patriots believed that the hoped-for Home Rule for Ireland would bring about an improvement in existing conditions.

The already tense situation was complicated by the determination of the people of the North to resist any question of control by the

South. This led to the formation of the Ulster Volunteers and the importation of firearms. Not unnaturally, perhaps, the men of the Southern counties (having watched the authorities turn a blind eye to the blatant gun-running), imported rifles themselves and began drilling.

The two foremost organizations in Southern Ireland were the Dublin-based Irish Citizen Army and the Irish National Volunteers. The aim of the Citizen Army was to combat the Dublin police, who were using force to break up the meetings and marchings of Jim Larkin's Irish Transport and General Workers' Union, and in the beginning the Army furnished itself with sticks, broom-handles (sometimes with a bayonet lashed to them, according to O'Casey in *Drums Under the Windows*) and heavy 'hurley sticks' (sticks used in an Irish form of hockey). Starvation often forced members of the Citizen Army to ask to return to work; they were usually refused. This caused many of them to join the second organization, at that time called the Irish National Volunteers, who were far more formidably armed. This group included many anti-labour members and had its own boy scout movement, with which the Countess Markiewicz was connected. She was one of the leaders of the Citizen Army, was married to a Polish nobleman, and fell out with O'Casey. Another prominent figure in the Volunteers was Padraic Pearse, and he was accompanied by members of Douglas Hyde's Gaelic League, and others involved in the movement known as Sinn Fein ('we ourselves'), which called upon Irishmen to rely upon themselves, not others, if they were to become independent.

With Home Rule promised for 1917, numbers of armed Irishmen, for or against it, were openly drilling and training to attack each other and the existing government – and this while World World I (1914–18) was being fought! Almost to a man the Ulster Volunteers enlisted in the British Army and formed the great Ulster Division that was shattered in the tremendous attack on Thiepval in 1916. A large number of the Irish National Volunteers also joined up; there was the same eagerness to enlist as in most parts of Britain.

Those who did not enlist, however, changed their name to the 'Irish Volunteers', asserting that England's difficulty was Ireland's opportunity. They decried the recruiting campaign that urged the

Irish Catholics to go to the rescue of Catholic Belgium, which was under immediate threat from the German forces. And they continued to drill determinedly, as did the Citizen Army (which had never wanted to be anything but a unit of the working class, and would not take up arms in any but a class war until they united with the Volunteers).

By 1916 the two groups had equipped themselves to a certain extent with uniforms: grey-green for the Volunteers, green for the Citizen Army; the idea being that if – or rather when – they declared Irish independence and were compelled to fight, they could claim rights as combatants under the Geneva Convention. Those without uniforms were to wear distinguishing armbands. O'Casey pointed out that they would be rebels in time of war – traitors, in effect – and he also warned them that troops would not hesitate to use artillery against them, no matter how much property was damaged. His warnings were ignored.

Strangely, no action was taken by the police during the 'manoeuvres' against Dublin Castle; admittedly, the civil authority did not wish to call in the military (though they had a perfect right to) in case awkward situations arose.

A decision was made to proclaim independence on Easter Monday 1916. Originally it was intended that the date should be earlier, and the rising was supposed to be general; but at the last moment telegrams were sent throughout the country to cancel all but the Dublin insurrection. Easter Monday was chosen, apparently, because most of the Dubliners would be at the seaside, the races – anywhere but in the middle of the city. A large supply of firearms was expected from Germany. This was to be landed and distributed under the direction of Sir Roger Casement, an Anglo-Irishman who loathed England and who had attempted to persuade Irish prisoners of war in Germany to form a legion to fight the British. The ship carrying the firearms was intercepted, however, and scuttled. Casement, who had been landed from a German submarine, was captured and later tried, convicted and executed.

The rebels marched to different points in Dublin to take up their positions. One party went to Dublin Castle, the headquarters of the police and Army Intelligence, and demanded admittance, which was refused by an unarmed policeman; they shot him and then made off.

The Citizen Army built a barricade on St Stephen's Green (they later moved elsewhere), and one of their early actions was to kill a carter who wished to remove his cart from the barricade. Padraic Pearse and other leaders took up their station in the Post Office in O'Connell Street, hastily fortified it, and from outside made the proclamation of independence. While this was happening De Valera established his headquarters at Boland's bakery (or Boland's Mills). They then waited to be attacked.

O'Casey has one of his characters in *The Plough and the Stars* refer to an attack on the Post Office by cavalry armed with lances and carbines, which was repulsed by the Volunteers; another account insists that the cavalry were armed only with sabres, were escorting some wagons to Phoenix Park, and knew nothing of the uprising until they were fired upon.

Soon the troops were called in to support the civil power. They found themselves fighting against their own countrymen, who occupied strong buildings from behind which they could snipe effectively. Not surprisingly, artillery was called in (as O'Casey had predicted) and the fighting continued for some days. A somewhat bizarre occurrence was the shelling of Liberty Hall (headquarters of the Citizen Army) by the Fisheries Protection vessel *Helga* – for the building's only occupant was a very startled caretaker. Eventually the decision was taken by the Army to burn the buildings round the rebel positions, thus compelling them to surrender.

While the fighting went on there was a good deal of looting by those who were not involved: small wonder, in view of the abject poverty in which most of them barely lived. The rebel leaders were rapidly tried and convicted; sixteen were executed before the British Government could intervene. The leader of the Citizen Army, already severely wounded, had to be carried to the firing-post. The executions angered many English people, who were by no means as vindictive as the anti-English propaganda would have the world believe; but the executions still resulted in the majority of the Irish (many of whom opposed the rebels) transferring their hatred to the British.

The whole episode was a tragedy and one can only imagine the feelings of those actively involved. It seems that the leaders of the rising demanded a blood-sacrifice (see the speech of the orator in Act 2 of *The Plough and the Stars*). It seems also that those not participating were frequently outraged by the actions of the insurgents; after all, 400,000 Irishmen joined the British Army, most of them from the South, and many Irish were mourning their own dead in World War I.

The British troops in Ireland were a mixture of inexperienced men and those well-tried in the trenches of France; they suddenly found themselves fighting an enemy who employed, for example, dum-dum bullets (see Note on Act 4). W. B. Yeats ended his poem *Easter 1916* with the words, 'A terrible beauty is born.' Maybe, but the birth pangs were frightful, the midwife's fee immense: 1,351 people were killed, seriously wounded, or maimed for life; 179 buildings in the heart of Dublin were mined, burned, or ransacked by looters; and at the end of the rising one-third of the population was on public relief.

Between the 1916 rising and that of 1920 (of *The Shadow of a Gunman*) the Irish feeling against the English had hardened; violent actions, in particular against the Royal Irish Constabulary, had spread throughout the country. Irish hopes had been raised to some extent by the Lloyd-George Convention of 1917, and were reinforced by Sinn Fein gains in the first post-war election. In addition, there had been a threat before the end of the war to extend conscription to Ireland. American money continued to find its way into the rebels' pockets, arms were smuggled and British troops were fired upon.

The negotiations between the British government and the Irish Nationalists are too complicated to be considered here, but a good deal was happening to affect the working-class populace of Dublin. The Royal Irish Constabulary lived in barracks; though they carried firearms they were not under discipline. They were not stationed in their home areas; the barracks were easily besieged; regular patrols easily ambushed; and local feeling was swiftly aroused against them. Consequently their morale suffered and they resigned in large numbers. Help was badly needed: the force was reorganized and a Dublin division added; hence the appearance there of an armed para-military police force, which often found itself at variance with the soldiers who had been called in.

Dublin was in a disturbed state. The Volunteers, who had been formed with the help of the secret society known as the Irish Republican Brotherhood, considered themselves to be the army of the as yet non-existent republic. The IRA had come into being; its members shot detectives and detectives shot its members, but the IRA received much sympathy from the poorer members of the public living in the rookeries where the gunman often hid. There were two reasons for this: first, the romantic feeling for the rebel, the bold Irish boy; and second, the fear of reprisals if help were not given.

The IRA was a terrorist organization, so it had to strike fear not only into the hearts of its enemies but also into the hearts of the general population. Gunmen did not hesitate to punish or eliminate any of their number who disobeyed orders; they also claimed to be enforcers of law in the districts where they lived. They set up local courts and administered 'justice' as they thought fit – their powers are reflected in Mr Gallogher's pathetic letter in *The Shadow of a Gunman*.

Faced with this situation, the authorities advertised for volunteers for the Royal Irish Constabulary in order to bolster its depleted numbers. They pay was good and so, naturally, was the response. Partly uniformed in khaki, with the black leather accoutrements of the RIC, they soon became known as the 'Black and Tans'; the government was even accused (unjustifiably) of clearing out the prisons in order to fill RIC ranks.

Soon after the formation of the first 'Tan' group the 'Auxiliaries' were added to them, their function being that of a flying column which would swiftly arrive on the scene of any incident or outbreak. Both these groups were rough, often heavy drinking, and inclined to abuse the public, both verbally and physically. They became detested in England as well as in Ireland. They were operating in a hostile environment against an invisible enemy on its own ground, and were virtually uncontrolled. What is evident is that these groups and the IRA operated a reign of terror against each other in which the ordinary citizen, whether republican or loyalist, was caught up and suffered the most in 'The Troubles'.

The Shadow of a Gunman

Plot and Themes

Plot

The plot of *The Shadow of a Gunman* is straightforward, though because of the nature of events the student is advised to read the foregoing 'Background' carefully.

Davoren is lodging with Seumas Shields, and is thought by the tenement dwellers to be an IRA gunman on the run from the troops. He is in fact a dreamer and a poet, who has led a hard life but has little capacity for action. Because of his supposed situation, he attracts to him the dissatisfied (Mrs Henderson and Mr Gallogher); romantic patriots (Minnie Powell); and those who will never do anything but talk (Tommy Owens, Adolphus Grigson). Ironically, a real member of the IRA, one Maguire, deposits a bag of Mills bombs in the room shared by Seumas and Davoren, then gets himself killed in an ambush at Knocksedan. This, and perhaps Tommy Owens's talking, leads to a raid, in which both Davoren and Seumas prove themselves to be inadequate frightened men, while Minnie, in order to draw suspicion from the 'gunman', takes the bombs, which are discovered by the soldiers in her room. She is herself taken out, and when the lorry is ambushed she is shot and dies. Seumas and Davoren are left to contemplate their own cowardice and the terrible reality – Seumas from his inherent superstitious viewpoint, Davoren with some new insight into himself and the nature of reality.

Themes

The themes of *The Shadow of a Gunman* are self-evident to a student of the play. Firstly, there is O'Casey's hatred of violence (and the fact that the innocent are always caught up in it). He is anti-war, anti-strife – themes which are to be more fully investigated in his later play, *The Silver Tassie*.

O'Casey's focus on the slum tenements (which were his own

inheritance) shows how greatly he deplores the living conditions which their inhabitants suffer; he underlines this by indicating that their only recourse is to drink and talk – escapes from their sordid day-to-day existence. O'Casey's treatment of this area of poverty is compassionate but wryly humorous as well, and one feels that his characters typify what are thought to be some traits of the Irish: laziness; garrulity; a tendency to be sentimental and break into song; a fervent patriotism (though not always in action); a sense of community; an inability to distinguish between the trivial and concerns of primary importance.

A sombre tone hangs over all; the events are localized yet have a universal importance, for they reflect man's inhumanity to man in the small compass and the large at the same time (remember that the play is set some two years after the end of World War I, and O'Casey is thus conveying a positive state of perspective). That poverty breeds war breeds tragedy is at the centre of O'Casey's thematic structure here, and though the church and religion are much cited they appear to exert little beneficent influence. The themes thus embrace the particular facet of events in Dublin historically, socially and morally, but they have universal significance.

Style

O'Casey's style is at once colloquial and poetic, displaying a remarkable facility and fluency (like that of his great predecessor Shakespeare), a control of idiom and dialect that embraces the use and abuse of words. His style ranges from the poetically sentimental to a vibrant economy in expressing the deep truths of poetry. The clarity of his own prose is shown in the stage directions and descriptions which precede each act, for example these words on Davoren: 'He bears upon his body the marks of the struggle for existence and the efforts towards self-expression.' But once we are in the play we note the variety of O'Casey's style, from the parody of romantic songs and sentiments as expressed in the lilting speech of Davoren, to the simple repetitions of the Irish brogue ('at all, at all').

The style is enriched by the width of O'Casey's reading – particularly in classical literature and English poetry – and is reflected in the expressions of Davoren and Seumas, though the colloquial is the ever-present language of men in their situation. Simple repetition is further extended in a parody of Irish speech habits, seen in the tendency to exaggerate, as when Davoren says 'And you actually rejoice and are exceedingly glad that . . .' At the same time, the simple speech sometimes carries a symbolic weight; such an instance occurs when Seumas's incompetence over his wares is shown in the wares themselves ('Oh, my God, there's the braces after breaking'). But the implication goes far beyond, and into the area of a greater 'breaking' – perhaps, in the words of Thomas Hardy, 'the breaking of nations'. Authenticity is conveyed by the use of slang and dialect expressions ('don't be trying to make a cod o' me') in the rich brogue of the class ('there's nothing I'm more fond of than a Hooley'). This is sometimes reinforced by a kind of Wilde-like witticism: 'A man should always be drunk, Minnie, when he talks politics – it's the only way in which to make them important' (Act 2, p.90).

Sometimes the word order, as is frequent in Irish speech, is partly reversed ('He has a few drinks taken'), while sometimes the brogue thickens into dialect in the fervour of the moment ('in the ardure ov me anger I disremembered there was a lady present'). But perhaps it would be fair to say that this kind of parody is never unkind; it merely conveys habits of speech in particular characters – witness Mr Gallogher, who speaks of the 'very identical room' and 'the very identical word', thus reflecting in the monotony of his speech the pathetic monotony of his existence. There is further pathos here in the high-flown style of Mr Gallogher's letter, where the language exists in complete contrast to ordinary speech, though it deals with an ordinary domestic row.

Sometimes the word-play reaches levels of sublimity and humour at one and the same time. Here is the magnificent Mrs Henderson in the course of two or three lines: 'For to be wise is to be a fool, an' to be a fool is to be wise', a statement that contains echoes of *Twelfth Night* and Feste's exchanges with Olivia. But here it is immediately followed by Mr Gallogher's 'Oh, Mrs Henderson, that a parrotox' which draws the rejoinder, 'It may be what a parrot talks...'; here the humour lies in the quality of the ignorance. In fact, Mrs Henderson's malapropisms are a kind of orchestration of the main theme: the misunderstanding and ignorance that come from the poverty in which she and her fellow cave-dwellers live.

Sometimes O'Casey injects a rhetorical style: see *The Plough and the Stars* for a superbly effective usage. Here it is in keeping with the character of Davoren, who sets the poet apart in some superb rhetorical flourishes: 'To them beauty is for sale in a butcher's shop. To the people the end of life is the life created for them; to the poet the end of life is the life that he creates for himself; life has a stifling grip upon the people's throat – it is the poet's musician' (Act 2, p.107).

O'Casey's style also includes a range of contemporary reference, which reinforces the authenticity. Thus Seumas can speak of the temptations of Minnie: 'jazz dances, fox-trots, picture theatres', as well as 'a British Tommy with a Mons Star'; two references that indicate the two worlds, of irresponsible escape on the one hand and war on the other.

The style also contains biblical echoes, perhaps because some of the characters, notably Seumas and Mrs Grigson, have somewhat voluble recourse to their religion. There is also the occasional vivid image: sudden, economic, effective; as when Seumas says that if the shooting continues, 'I'll be nothing but a galvanic battery of shocks'. Least effective stylistically is O'Casey's attempt to capture the English cockney dialect in the voice of the Auxiliary, for the distortion is such that although it is recognizable it is, one feels, a deliberately vicious caricature (koind blowke, sawr, prawse, for example) – and thus detracts from the immediate realism of the scene. The salient feature throughout is, however, the life of the language; and it is this that makes the play vibrant with force, comedy, threat and, ultimately, tragedy.

Characters

Davoren

There is in his face an expression that seems to indicate an eternal war between weakness and strength.

The above sentence is O'Casey's own key to the character of Davoren, the 'shadow' of the gunman who enjoys the romance and status of his supposed situation, and lacks therefore the basic integrity and honesty of purpose to speak out and kill rumour. As a result, he is indirectly responsible for another kind of killing – that of Minnie Powell, who believes in Davoren, thus ironically emphasizing by her fervent idealism his own lack of bravery and substance. O'Casey stresses the conflict in Davoren; the pendulum swinging between activity and rest. He has suffered much, and appears to be in another shadow, that of Shelley. He has the capacity to be completely absorbed in his writing, and is able to translate his love for Shelley into vivid contemporary relevance ('He flung a few stones through stained-glass windows'), but he loses patience with himself for having landed himself in the lodgings with Seumas. He grows used to the idea – proudly – that people think that he is a gunman on the run; it gives him the opportunity to take refuge in Shelley, and to compare himself with Prometheus!

Davoren's initial reception of Minnie is an uncertain one, and he even becomes a little pompous ('A man should always be drunk, Minnie, when he talks politics'), though there is a terrible irony in these words in view of the fact that Tommy Owens talks freely of Davoren in a pub. Davoren quotes a romantic song to Minnie (he always has quotations at his fingertips), and responds to her warmth and attractiveness, being secretly delighted when she tells him that he is 'a gunman on the run'. He has a somewhat ironic attitude towards a patriotic death, as he reveals in his remark about Robert Emmet. But he is fluttered and flattered by the attention his supposed role affords him, and indulges himself with thoughts of bravery and triumphant reactions, becoming almost devil-may-care in his attitude ('a gunman throws a bomb as carelessly as a schoolboy throws a snowball').

Davoren is very taken with Minnie, seeing himself as a 'pioneer in action, as I am a pioneer in thought'. Just as he is about to kiss her, Tommy Owens interrupts, and Davoren is moved to state that he has nothing to do either with the Republic or with politics. Mrs Henderson and Mr Gallogher further elevate his self-esteem, and despite the comic overtones of their belief in him we become increasingly aware of Davoren's misguided and vulnerable belief in himself. He is overcome, stricken with timidity again, by the exuberance of the Henderson–Gallogher verbosity, and is shocked, temporarily, by the shouted news of Maguire's death. But his thoughts soon return romantically to Minnie, his curtain speech at the end of Act 1 lifting him into a kind of delusive self-confidence ('And what danger can there be in being the shadow of a gunman?').

Act 2 finds him, Shelley-like, invoking the moon; he is supremely aware of beauty and ugliness; in an exchange with Seumas, he elevates poetry above people. Warned by Seumas about Minnie, Davoren praises her. He also boasts of his acceptance of death and his belief in his own philosophy. But as the situation worsens, he wishes he were not there. He is impatient with the loquacious Mrs Grigson, even more so with the drunken singing of Mr Grigson. He is fearful that he will not find the Gallogher letter (in order to destroy it), and even more frightened when he discovers the Mills bombs. This increases his wish to leave, and his philosophy is now in abeyance. As the door is nearly broken down, he 'reclines almost fainting on the bed'. He is cowardly and abject in the face of interrogation. He curses Mr Grigson when he finds that the latter has brought home whisky and that the soldiers have got it. He acknowledges his cowardice when both he and Seumas pray that Minnie will keep her mouth shut. He also makes a 'sickly attempt at humour', but when the noise of the ambush is heard he cowers down out of the way. His conscience is moved by Minnie's death, and finds it 'still more terrible to think that Davoren and Shields are alive'.

'Poltroon and poet' Davoren calls himself at the end. But the heavy irony is that just as he has been the shadow of a gunman he is also a shadow of a poet and in effect a shadow of a man. He thinks he is detached, a poet set apart, but – through vanity and cowardice – he is unable to sustain his philosophy. Davoren never reaches the poetic mountain-top; and he is brought down to a terrible reality by Minnie's death. He has been a self-indulgent and ineffectual dreamer who has tried to withdraw from the human and humane responsibilities of life.

Seumas Shields

In him is frequently manifested the superstition, the fear and the malignity of primitive man.

Seumas acts as a commentary or chorus on the main action of the play and in reaction to the situations it provides. Almost his first words emphasize this: 'the Irish people are still in the stone age. If they could they'd throw a bomb at you.' He is lazy, a man of inaction, a pedlar by trade, full of delays and talk, but he has picked up much heterogeneous information and not a little wisdom. He mocks the pretentiousness of Davoren's absorption in poetry, but displays a knowledge of poetry himself. He nevertheless prefers religion to poetry, asserting that, 'I rejoice in the vindication of the Church and Truth.' His slovenliness is epitomized by the fact that he feels he doesn't need to wash himself, makes a great show of checking his wares, while the breaking of the braces has an almost symbolic resonance in the play. He reminisces in a heartfelt way about his services to the Irish Republican Brotherhood, but is not without a certain insight; for example when he says, 'That's the Irish people all over – they treat a joke as a serious thing and a serious thing as a joke.'

Seumas has, in fact, acquired a great deal of knowledge: he has taught Irish [just as O'Casey did] and he is able to cap most of Davoren's quotations with additions or associations of his own. He is in some ways independent and aggressive – writing letters to the papers (according to his landlord), thus exposing slum conditions and unscrupulous profiteering. He refers to the tenements rightly as a 'rookery', but his most original contribution – echoed again in the play [and in the third volume of O'Casey's *Drums Under the Windows: Autobiography*, Volume 3] – is, 'Oh, Kathleen ni Houlihan, your way's a thorny way.'

The death of Maguire finds Seumas's inherent selfishness confirmed: he thinks of his possessions that Maguire had, and frets about not getting them back. He can't sleep because of the curfew, he says, and engages Davoren in a discussion about poetry, asserting that, 'I think a poet's claim to greatness depends upon his power to put passion in the common people.' His superstitious nature is shown in his reaction when he hears the tapping, which is 'a sure sign of death'. He speaks out about Minnie Powell, again showing the paradox of his culture when, for example, he calls her 'A Helen of Troy come to live in a tenement', with Davoren as 'a kind o' Paris'.

Seumas reveals that he has outgrown patriotism and the rule of the gun, asserting that the Irish can't defeat the British Empire. He is wise in his appraisal of the futility of it all, and he has a forecasting imagination, pointing out that in the fighting it's the civilians who suffer. Once again he says that he gets his own comfort from religion, but the more frightened he becomes the more he repeats himself, acquiring a kind of longish conversational stutter, further bewailing the state of the country. He is thrown into a panic by the discovery of the Mills bombs in the bag left by Maguire, and (for fear of incriminating himself) attempts to deny his knowledge that Maguire was connected with the Republican movement. He is afraid of what will be found in Minnie's room, and spends much of his time praying that she will keep her mouth shut.

Seumas is intent on saving himself, telling Davoren to keep quiet, in case he may be heard. He realizes that the innocent will suffer, and covers his own cowardice by a show of telling Grigson how he has treated the Auxiliary. When Minnie dies, Seumas refuses to be involved, saying that 'she did it off her own bat'. His own remark (the last lines of the play), implying that the tapping had portended death, stresses his essentially superstitious nature. He is, nevertheless, a curious mixture of self-preservation and good sense.

Minnie Powell

She is a girl of twenty-three, but the fact of being forced to earn her living . . . has given her a force and an assurance beyond her years.

Minnie is an attractive, impulsive and forthright girl, caught up in romantic idealism and its practical application. Her heart rules her head. She dresses well and becomingly, enhancing her own appearance, and this in Davoren's eyes compensates for her lack of education. She assumes but little disguise for her own motives – nominally coming to see Davoren in order to borrow some milk, but in reality already interested in him. In any case, she doesn't like being on her own. Davoren's literary references pass over her head; she cares for dancing and having a good time. But she has an intensely Republican spirit which is later to shame the menfolk. She believes what she wants to believe about Davoren, telling him 'it's time to give up the writing an' take to the gun'. She behaves roguishly when Davoren sings a romantic song, ingratiates herself with him, and offers to run in and tidy up for him.

Minnie is what other women would consider 'forward'; but she asserts her own independence, saying that she has had to push hard in life and that she intends to do what she wants to do. But she is, of course, sentimental and romantic, and asks Davoren to type his name and hers together. She lets him kiss her. Minnie's great moment comes when she takes the bag with the Mills bombs to her room. She belies Seumas's opinion of her, enjoys sacrificing herself to save Davoren; but she actually dies in an ambush. She is in love with the idea of the romantic hero, and sees clearly the role she must play in relation to him. In terms of courage and the ability to act, Minnie puts the men to shame.

Other characters

Virtually all the other characters in *The Shadow of a Gunman* are caricatures, and most of them contribute to the comedy underlying the sombre theme. *Mrs Henderson* is admirably described by O'Casey and exists to dominate *Mr Gallogher* and the company generally. The pair are a comedy team, for she is making use of her personality to visit the gunman, and asserting the right of the IRA to bring about domestic as well as national order – a rather grotesque interpretation, yet one that underlines, perhaps, the state of insecurity and the lack of civil law and order. Mr Gallogher is an admirable foil, and his letter is a masterpiece of pedantic and pompous utterance – again with the comic element uppermost. The idea of appealing to the IRA to settle domestic problems strikes a sardonic note of which both the characters involved are unaware.

Tommy Owens – representing the essential garrulity and the extremes of verbal patriotism – finds, like Minnie, an admirable focus for them in the presence of Davoren. He drinks too much and talks too much, so that he is bound to talk in an unguarded way about the gunman. Like other O'Casey characters of his class and attitude, he frequently breaks into song.

Mr Grigson complements Tommy in some ways – he talks too much, he boasts too much, he drinks too much. But whereas Tommy is by any standards a pathetic figure, Grigson, with his self-importance, his language and whisky to cover his fear, demonstrates that the older foolish people get, the more stupid and obdurate in their ways do they become. Fortunately, or perhaps unfortunately, he has an indulgent and pathetic wife who spoils him and cares only for his safety. Naturally, he is as incapable as the other men in the play, but provides more of the comic current – particularly when his wife describes him as sitting up in bed pathetically singing while the auxiliaries drink his whisky.

The Auxiliary is rough, crude, ignorant, but cunning enough to have an eye for the main chance; the word whisky takes him away from his responsibilities to the place where it is to be found.

The Landlord, too, is self-seeking, but in a different way; he will abuse Seumas, but is wary of his 'guests'. His eye is on future events, and doubtless he will be on the winning side. O'Casey's characters are convincing, particularly in their use (and misuse) of idiom and dialect.

Act summaries and textual notes

Act 1

This Act opens with an elaborate description of the setting which stresses its incongruity with the nature of its occupants. This is exemplified in the description of the character of Donal Davoren, whose 'struggle through life has been a hard one', although he has a 'belief in the redemption of all things by beauty everlasting'. Seumas Shields is an effective contrast, representing 'the superstition, the fear and the malignity of primitive man'.

Davoren is singing, while shouts from the door and window are intended to rouse Seumas from his bed. There is a certain comic flavour in Seumas's not hearing the noise (or rather his affectation of not hearing it), and in Davoren's absorption in his poetry. Seumas reveals that he has been expecting Maguire, who has ordered him to be ready and packed. The two argue briefly, Seumas perhaps representing, in his own muddled personality, the chaos of Ireland at that time. At this point, Maguire enters in haste; he reveals that he is going to catch butterflies at Knocksedan (what he is really doing is revealed later). Seumas considers that this is irresponsible and typical of the country of Ireland. Then Mulligan the landlord enters, to the obvious resentment of Seumas, who owes him the eleven weeks' rent he has come to collect. Mulligan serves notice to quit on Seumas and threatens to evict him, while Davoren regrets his own decision to stay in this kind of house, where there is no peace for a poet to work. When Mulligan has gone, Seumas tells Davoren that the landlord and many others think that he, Davoren, is 'on the run' (remember that this phrase was the original title of the play). Seumas leaves, and Minnie Powell enters. Again O'Casey provides a full description of his heroine. She has come ostensibly for some milk, but in reality to talk and to make up to Davoren; she tells him – perhaps wilfully misunderstanding him because she wants to – 'It's to give up the writing now an' take to the gun.' She even misinterprets a sentimental poem he quotes, but Davoren becomes 'susceptible to the attractiveness of Minnie', and she obviously believes that he is a 'gunman on the run'; he is too flattered to tell her the truth about himself. The romance develops quickly, but just as Davoren is about to kiss Minnie, Tommy Owens (small, weedy, hero-worshipping), enters. He is garrulous; he, too, obviously thinks that Davoren is a gunman, and ignores Davoren's assertion that he knows nothing about politics. Tommy's non-stop talking and innuendo greatly embarrass Minnie – and he says that he would die for Ireland if the opportunity arose, believing that everyone should be out with the IRA.

Tommy's fervent patriotic flow is interrupted by the entrance of the massive Mrs Henderson, accompanied by the far from dominating Mr Gallogher. After giving Davoren an account of the residents in the back drawing-room who are making Mr Gallogher's life a misery, Mrs Henderson urges Gallogher to read aloud a letter he has brought with him. His pompous comic letter is read out, and Davoren is consulted as to the actual wording; the ridiculous nature of the scene is underlined by the running humour of the fact that Davoren is not the important gunman they think he is. In a sombre play this appeal to the IRA to intervene in a domestic squabble (does this symbolize the wider domestic squabble?) carries a grotesque overtone.

Mrs Henderson continues with her own abuse of language – she is a kind of Irish Mrs Malaprop. Suddenly, outside, a newsboy is heard, and we learn that there has been an ambush at Knocksedan and that a man called Maguire has been killed. Despite this, Davoren and Minnie continue their romantic exchanges; finally Davoren is left alone on stage, asking himself the question, 'What danger can there be in being the shadow of a gunman?'

A Return Room An extra room added to a tenement.

the might of design . . . beauty everlasting The quotation is from lines spoken by Louis Dubedat in G. B. Shaw's *The Doctor's Dilemma*, which obviously influenced O'Casey in his concept of Davoren.

Or when sweet Summer's ardent arms outspread Note the romantic, escapist tone of this poetry: imitation Shelley, well removed from reality. Davoren is going to be forced into *real* experience soon.

at all, at all Standard Irish colloquial repetition, often used to caricature Irish speech and make it humorous.

bedlam i.e. a madhouse. (A corruption of 'Bethlehem', from Bethlehem Hospital, used since 1547 as an insane asylum.)

oul' ones bawl at a body i.e. old people shout at one.

Morpheus God of dreams in Greek mythology.

Somnus The god of Sleep and brother of Death, hence an ironic reference, and part of Seumas's varied knowledge.

The poppy was his emblem The milky juice of the poppy (i.e. opium) has narcotic properties.

The Angelus The bell ringing for Roman Catholic devotional exercise at morning, noon and sunset.

a rap i.e. a knock (on the door).

Kathleen ni Houlihan Synonymous with Ireland and hence identified with patriotism that involves suffering for the cause; hence the 'thorny way'.

Ah me! alas, pain . . . for ever Shelley's *Prometheus Unbound* was published in 1820. Prometheus stole fire from heaven, and was chained as a result. This is line 23 of Act 1 of Shelley's drama, and is repeated at line 30, thus having the same rhetorical effect as it has here in O'Casey's play.

He flung a few stones Probably a reference to Shelley's known atheism, the reason for his expulsion from Oxford.

a jazz dance Remember that the setting of the play is May 1920, and the early twenties of this century came to be known as The Jazz Age.

Black and Tans See section on 'Background'.

there's great stuff i.e. they are well made.

Cuchullian A great Irish legendary hero (also spelt Cuchulain).

Keep your hair on i.e. don't get excited.

blew in i.e. came to see you.

Knocksedan In County Dublin.

to catch butterflies An innocent-sounding occupation covering a practical reality.

a cod i.e. a fool.

did i.e. done.

all the butterflies might be dead A continuation of the innocent-sounding phrase – but here evocative of death; thus ironic in view of what happens to Maguire.

a Gael An Irishman (of the original stock).

knocking about now i.e. living at the present time.

the Irish Republican Brotherhood See section on 'Background'.

rifle levy i.e. a contribution towards the purchase of arms.

James Stephens (1824–1901); active in the Fenian cause in Ireland

and America; arrested in Dublin but escaped and then gradually ceased to be of importance.

Pro-Cathedral The main Roman Catholic Church of Dublin.

Dark Rosaleen A symbol of Ireland distressed, from 'Dark Rosaleen', a poem by James Clarence Mangan (1803–49).

good-bye . . . ee An echo of a line from one of the popular songs of the First World War.

Balor of the Evil Eye In Celtic mythology, a sea-giant, one of whose eyes had the power of destroying whatever it looked upon.

a half tall hat In general shape, like those worn at weddings and at Ascot, but much lower in the crown.

be i.e. by.

gostherin' Talking idly, gossiping.

Ah me! alas, pain, pain Again, the lines from *Prometheus Unbound*.

green, white, an' yellow Significant colours in terms of Irish patriotism.

billickin' i.e. bilking – not paying money owed.

Be me sowl i.e. upon my soul.

troglodytes i.e. cave-dwellers (they lived in the cellars of the slums).

blow i.e. complain.

Got the wind up i.e. is scared.

rookery i.e. a crowded tenement.

Fury One of the goddesses of Greek mythology sent by Tartarus to punish crime.

tam o' shanter Round woollen or cloth cap, full in the crown but fitting closely round brows.

lashins i.e. more than enough.

a Hooley An entertainment, with dancing.

I danced rings round me This is Minnie's way of describing her ecstatic participation in the dance.

two-pair back i.e. the rooms at the back of the tenement, on the second storey.

melodeon A small organ with suction-operated reeds, a kind of accordion.

Orpheus In Greek mythology, he was known for his entrancing music, hence the reference here.

weeshy Very small, tiny.

dawny Weakly, sickly, delicate.

bit of a man i.e. of poor physique.

A man should always be drunk Note the balance of this witticism, almost reminiscent of the humour and cleverness of Oscar Wilde.

jars i.e. glasses of liquor; usually refers to beer.
an' the men o' '98 The United Irishmen, who rebelled in 1798.
oul' weeds i.e. flowers. Remember that Minnie is very much the tenement girl with no knowledge of nature.
One day, when Morn's Again a typical quotation, romantic and sentimental, but underlining the reality to come, which contrasts so tellingly with this escapist verse.
coddin' i.e. fooling me, misleading me.
Annie Laurie wasn't the sweetheart of Bobbie Burns Robert Burns (1759–96) was the celebrated Scots poet. Annie Laurie of the popular Scottish ballad was in real life the mother of the hero in Burns's poem 'The Whistle'.
Robert Emmet (1778–1803); a patriotic Irishman born in Dublin who was hanged for his part in attempting to seize Dublin Castle.
the ambushes Again ironic, since Minnie is to die in one.
excited emotions ... frightened at the suggestion Note that this implies sexual timidity in Davoren, another instance of his fear of reality.
grasp this sorry scheme of things Note again that Davoren has recourse to poetry.
He has a few drinks taken An echo of the way Tommy would speak, with this description having its own humorous innuendo.
dungarees Overalls (usually of denim).
minded i.e. cared about.
There's no flies on Tommy i.e. he's sharp, he doesn't miss anything.
burgeons Minnie means burdens, but malapropisms are a commonplace in this play.
Up the Republic i.e. long live the Republic!
a nod's as good as a wink to a blind horse i.e. you have no need to say anything – we understand – it's all the same to us.
pro nor con For or against.
Two firm hands clasped together Another quotation from a patriotic song, and Tommy continues in verse as is the custom of his race!
hayros i.e. heroes.
Ayryinn i.e. Ireland (mispronunciation of 'Erin').
he also serves who only stands and waits An adaptation of the last line of Milton's celebrated sonnet *On His Blindness*: 'They also serve who only stand and wait.'
the I.R.A. See references in the section on 'Background'.
as Sarsfield said at the battle o' Vinegar Hill There was a battle

there in 1798 (near Wexford) where the Southern contingent of United Irishmen were defeated. Patrick Sarsfield was a supporter of James II.

an' a penny buys a whistle Tommy means that you get what you pay for.

ardure ov i.e. ardour of.

disremembered i.e. forgot.

wan ov i.e. one of.

ov the people . . . by the people Mrs Henderson's statement here of the democratic ideal is (roughly) taken from the famous Gettysburg address of November 1863 by the United States president Abraham Lincoln (1809–65): '. . . government of the people, by the people, and for the people, shall not perish from the earth.'

nor i.e. than.

there's game in Mr Gallicker still i.e. he's still got life and vitality.

cock Look.

we know our own know i.e. we know what we know. The implication is that they all know that Davoren is a gunman.

fairity i.e. truthfulness, honesty.

the very identical The very same. The word 'identical' is a favourite of Gallogher's, and its use here is part of O'Casey's verbal humour at the expense of Irish speech.

these tramps' cleverality i.e. the cunning of your disreputable neighbours.

decomposed Mrs Henderson merely means 'composed', but she is trying to sound impressive.

top sayin' i.e. the form of address.

swank Showing off.

Republican Courts i.e. set up by the IRA.

foreign Courts i.e. the British.

childer i.e. children.

be i.e. by.

aforesaid defendant i.e. who will have to defend himself against my charges. Note the pseudo-legal tone.

Primmy Fashy Case i.e. prima facie: at first sight, based on the first impression.

this tenth day of the fifth month Notice that this makes nonsense of the other date mentioned at the beginning of the letter.

Sinn Fein Amhain A reference to the meaning of 'Sinn Fein': 'we ourselves'.

sowl-case Slang for 'the body'.

'clare i.e. declare.

to make a jeer ov him i.e. mocking and ridiculing him.
mallavogin' i.e. a good telling off.
For to be wise is to be a fool, an' to be a fool is to be wise An echo of Feste's dialogue with Olivia in Shakespeare's *Twelfth Night.*
parrotox i.e. a paradox.
got a make Got any money.
Yis Yes.
hans Hands.
particularated i.e. particularized.
mandamus A judicial writ issued from the Queen's Bench division as command to inferior court.
interpretate i.e. interpret.
supernally One suspects that he means either 'personally'; or even, since he uses high-flown language, 'superlatively'.
Faith ov our Fathers . . . Wrap the Green Flag Roun me Patriotic nationalistic songs.
only waits the call i.e. to serve his country.
And what danger can there be Ironic, since the danger is to others, the innocent ones caught up in his situation.

Act 2

The setting is as for Act 1, but it is night, and Maguire's bag has, significantly, been left where it was. Davoren continues with his Shelley-like poetry, and he and Seumas discuss Maguire, Seumas bemoaning the fact that he will never get certain things back from Maguire. Seumas attacks poetry, Davoren defends it, and in return attacks the people. Seumas thinks he hears tapping, which in his mind presages evil; something bad about to happen. Eventually Davoren goes to bed, and Seumas criticizes Minnie Powell and the way that she has attached herself to Davoren; the latter tells him to leave off. Seumas, who can't sleep, observes that 'The country has gone mad'; he obviously deplores the existing state of violence, more particularly the state of Ireland. He stresses his belief that the British Army cannot be defeated, and that it is the civilians who get injured – an ironic/prophetic anticipation of what is to come.

Seumas asserts that there is a great comfort in religion, but while they are talking they hear a volley of shots. Seumas thinks that bombs are being manufactured in the stables nearby. Then Mrs

Grigson, 'one of the cave-dwellers of Dublin' enters; she has been sitting up waiting for the return of her husband who, she fears, may have been shot by the Black and Tans. Again we are aware of the grim humour underlying the situation, for she wants to know if the insurance company would pay up if her husband were to be shot after curfew. Shortly after this Mr Grigson stumbles into the room; he talks loudly, and is obviously somewhat drunk. He tells Davoren that he (Grigson) is not an informer; he takes another drink and then breaks into song. Meanwhile those in the room hear a 'rapidly moving motor' approaching the house. This has the effect of throwing them into a state of fear, and Grigson reveals that he has heard Tommy Owens talking in a pub about Davoren. The latter is searching for Gallogher's letter which, he remembers, is addressed to the Irish Republican Army, and could therefore prove embarrassing or incriminating if found by the Auxiliaries. Now shots are heard outside; Davoren finds the letter, and he and Seumas then make an even more incriminating discovery: Maguire's bag is full of Mills bombs! They try desperately to think what would be best to do, and at this point Minnie Powell enters dramatically. Her entrance is followed by a banging on the door. Minnie sees that Davoren and Seumas are in a panic, and takes the bag herself, saying that the soldiers won't do anything to a girl. After she has left, one of the Auxiliaries enters the room and examines Davoren and Seumas. They also search the Grigsons, and Mrs Grigson recounts how they have thrown a Bible on the floor. Minnie's voice is heard shouting 'Up The Republic' as she is taken away; but later she is shot and killed as the lorry she is in is ambushed. Only the cowards are saved; and Seumas and Davoren are left with their thoughts – in Davoren's case a recognition, perhaps, of the terrible reality from which he has run away, by being the poet on the 'mountain-top'.

The cold chaste moon The moon is often used metaphorically by poets to represent coldness and chastity.
two of them i.e. bullets.
I'm to sing dumb i.e. keep quiet.
they put on this damned curfew i.e. compelling people to be in their houses by a certain time every evening.

the pearly glint of the morning dew Seumas is, of course, mocking the escapist and sentimental type of poetry favoured by Davoren.

They live in the abyss Davoren here asserts his essential beliefs. In a sense, they are as high-flown as Mr Gallogher's letter and they prove to be divorced from the reality he is soon to experience.

Whisht Listen!

there's always something ... one of our family dies Note how this underlies the superstitious element in Seumas's nature.

God between us an' all harm i.e. may God protect us from injury.

fox-trots Popular dance at the time.

picture theatres i.e. cinemas.

Education has been wasted ... primitive instincts Ironic, in view of the instincts Seumas has just displayed and the instinct for self-survival that Davoren is to show.

A Helen of Troy ... Paris Helen left her husband Menelaus and eloped with Paris, thus bringing about the Greeks' ten year siege of Troy.

gaddin' i.e. having a good time with.

I do not mourn me darlin' lost Obviously another quotation from a popular patriotic song.

Tricoloured Ribbon O Orange, white and green.

a British Tommy with a Mons Star i.e. a British soldier who had fought at the battle of Mons (in Belgium) in 1914 against the Germans.

and they were all over forty An indication of the tension in Davoren with this vicious implication that adults often behave like children.

The village cock hath thrice Although Seumas is quite accurate in his identification of the quotation and where it comes from, the line should read 'The early village-cock/Hath twice done salutation to the morn'.

paternosters i.e. the Lord's Prayer.

De Profundis Cry from the depths of sorrow (Psalm 130).

The Soldiers' Song Adopted as the Irish National Anthem in 1937, it was written c. 1917; words by Patrick Kenney, music by Patrick Heaney.

the gun almighty A straight adaptation from the Apostles' Creed used in the Christian Church.

plug i.e. shoot.

blowin' i.e. talking too much about.

communicant One who receives Holy Communion.

philosophy ... coward brave; the sufferer defiant Fine words, soon to be shown as shallow and meaningless when coming from Davoren.

but a galvanic battery o' shocks Seumas is not, at times, without a vivid and contemporary turn of phrase.

there I'll leave you i.e. I'll let you guess.
cave dwellers Remember the earlier reference to 'troglodytes'.
sign or light i.e. not a glimpse.
Black an' Tans See reference in the section on 'Background'.
a sup Quite a number of drinks.
too far gone . . . for that i.e. he is too old to change his ways now.
them Societies i.e. insurance companies.
mindin' you i.e. taking any notice of you.
there's no blottin' it out i.e. no denying it.
wasn't born in a bottle Perhaps a self-ironic reference to his own drinking habits.
A most appropriate place i.e. because he drinks.
fit to take a fall out av i.e. capable of mocking or bringing him down a peg or two.
goughers Cheats, swindlers.
deludin' Mrs Grigson too suffers from the malapropistic habit. She means 'alluding'.
in the letter an' in the spirit i.e. completely.
have you me Do you understand me?
an Orangeman A member of the society dedicated to establishing Protestant ascendancy in Ireland. It was founded in 1795.
Tone, Emmet an' Parnell The first founded the United Irishmen, and committed suicide in 1798; for the second, see note p.30; the third is the great Irish leader and Home Ruler (1846–91) who fell from power because of his affair with Kitty O'Shea.
King William i.e. William of Orange (1650–1702), King of England. He defeated the resistants at the Battle of the Boyne in 1690.
Hobah Black Chapter – that's my Lodge Presumably a reference to freemasonry.
The Orange Lily O Perhaps the Protestant equivalent of Kathleen ni Houlihan.
The Vic'roy i.e. Viceroy of Ireland.
Lady Clarke Wife of the Viceroy.
Connaught filly O i.e. horse bred and trained in that county.
a traneen A scrap, a straw (a reference to something worthless).
blowin' . . . little blower i.e. one who is always talking too much.
the Staff i.e. officers of the IRA.
Mills bombs Oval hand-grenades, named after the inventor.
St Anthony Patron saint of swineherds.
celerity Speed.
if they do aself If they do, anyway.

Tommies British soldiers.
awd Hard.
ay Eh?
koind blowke i.e. kind chap (sarcastic).
Deloighted i.e. delighted.
lingo i.e. language.
ahn Own.
sawr Saw.
abaht About.
prawse i.e. price.
ikey Cunning, clever.
curer i.e. nothing to relieve his hangover.
flitter i.e. scatter.
blaguards i.e. blackguards.
Submit yourselves Certainly the beginning of this is accurate, but Mrs Grigson makes her own additions towards the end.
Mr Moody an' Mr Sankey Two great American evangelists, who produced a strong effect on their visits to Great Britain in 1873 and 1883.
We shall meet in the Sweet Bye an' Bye A quotation from a very famous hymn, often associated with Evangelists and the Salvation Army.
sacret i.e. secret.
Auxsie i.e. the Auxiliary policeman; see 'Background'.
riddled Shot full of bullets.
after gettin' i.e. they have discovered.
a coolin' Probably equivalent – oddly – to a 'roasting' – make her suffer for what she has done.
pom-poms Ornamental tufts, or bunches of ribbon, worn on hats and shoes.
put a bother i.e. get (me) into a state, a panic.
have you me Do you understand what I mean?
blottin' it out i.e. denying it.
a stiff upper front Normally, a stiff upper lip, i.e. keep a brave face on things.
buzzom Bosom.
off her own bat On her own initiative.
an' some other name i.e. Davoren's.
till the silver cord i.e. until you die (Ecclesiastes, 12,6).

The Plough and the Stars

Plot and themes

Plot

Before reading the following notes on the plot, the student is advised to look closely at the section on 'Background' in order to get into perspective the events of November 1915, (which are covered in the first two acts) and the widely and immediately important happenings of Easter Week 1916.

Fundamentally the play is about the conflict of domestic and political loyalties, seen in Nora Clitheroe's relationship with her husband. He succumbs to pressures and is finally killed, the tragic irony of the plot lying in the fact that Nora has burned the letter which conveyed the news of his promotion to Commandant in the Citizen Army – the force he had previously left on her account. Fluther, The Covey and Peter, together with the prostitute Rosie, are almost a chorus on and reflection of the events of the times, while Bessie and Mrs Gogan are also seen in conflict. The plot thus exists on two levels: the effect of outside events on domestic lives; and the conflicts of those domestic lives seen as a comparable or contrasting movement.

Clitheroe rejoins the Army; his wife searches for him; he returns to her briefly with the dying Langoan; he leaves her again and is killed, proud to die for Ireland. Nora loses her baby; she is nursed by Bessie, who grows in stature as the tragedy unwinds; and the English soldiers arrive while the ordinary people are engaged in looting the shops. The soldiers hold Fluther, Peter and The Covey in one room with Bessie and Nora, but they are harassed by a sniper. Nora becomes demented and searches for her lost baby, reverts to the past after the death of her husband, and goes to the window. Bessie tries to pull her back from it, is shot and killed by the sniper. The English soldiers are left with the tea which Nora had made, and sing the song that typifies the sentimental and nostalgic in war – as against the terrible realism they are living through: 'Keep the 'owme fires burning'.

Themes

The themes are clear-cut. The play is an assault on the *conditions of the Irish slum-dwellers* (consider the death of Mollser as a direct result of these), and equally an assault on *violence* and the fact that *war catches the innocent* in its clutches. There is also a clearsighted look at the *degradation of human nature* that arises as the result of poverty and the uncertainties of the local situation – the selfishness, arguments, fighting on a domestic level echo the looting, misguided nationalism, political and emotive manoeuvring (witness the voice of the speaker). These themes are tragic in the widest sense, for they show the destruction of lives by social conditions, war and political blackmail.

O'Casey's love of human nature is such that the themes are expressed with a mixture of humorous and tragic insight, the laughter and tears that constitute life. The events in Dublin of 1915–16 give him the opportunity to express his fundamental belief that man is reducing himself by his inability to improve social conditions, and by his capacity to be misled by the rhetoric of politics and a spurious nationalism. And O'Casey sees, tragically and unequivocally, that it is the innocent who suffer.

Style

O'Casey's style in *The Plough and the Stars* is as varied as in *The Shadow of a Gunman*, and his *scene-setting* and *descriptions* are as full as in the earlier play. Thus Peter Flynn has 'a face shaped like a lozenge', while Mrs Gogan has 'an insinuating manner and sallow complexion'. The Irish brogue is particularly thick in this play – which is full of dialect and colloquialisms – and the 'th' is particularly prominent ('mysthery' and 'thrimmin'). The *speech* is the speech of the working class of the period, in the Dublin tenements O'Casey knew so well. It is, consequently, racy in terms of image, of cliché and vivid slang, all at the same time; for example 'but when you get his goat, or he has a few jars up, he's vice versa'. Sometimes there is a curious interjection of *learning*, particularly in the references of The Covey, and in addition there is the layer of religious reference that one finds in the speech of Bessie.

Song is used throughout, the sentimental and nostalgic lilt of Clitheroe's song to Nora in the beginning taking on tragic overtones before the end when it is re-echoed by Nora herself in her demented state. A rich vein of *humour* runs throughout the play, as in the exchanges about 'The Sleepin' Vennis' between Peter, Fluther and Mrs Gogan. But equally impressive is the voice of the speaker which provides a kind of emotive call to arms and idealism which is at once spurious, repugnant and yet of course persuasive. If we consider these words:

> Bloodshed is a cleansing and sanctifying thing, and the nation that regards it as the final horror has lost its manhood. (Act 2)

It may be noted how superbly O'Casey has captured here the emotive and repellent *jargon* of the time – curiously, in his native Irish context, anticipating the Nazi tones and slanted invocations which were to come only a few years later. Fluther has some marvellous *idiom* which keeps down to earth by way of contrast; for instance when he says 'where th' slim thinkin' counthry boyo ud limp away from th' first faintest touch of compromization!' The Covey, on the other hand, repeats another kind of jargon, that which echoes a different kind of propaganda from the militaristic speaker, when he refers to 'th' war for th' economic emancipation of th' proletariat'.

Rosie can be even more down to earth, telling Fluther that 'If I was a man, or you were a woman, I'd bate th' puss o' you!' What might be called pure *Irish slang* is common when Fluther, Peter and The Covey are talking. There are some fine proverbial moments, as when The Covey observes, 'if everyone was blind you'd steal a cross off an ass's back!' Bessie's invocations are in the form of prayers to God, but the contrasting solace sought by the ignorant and unspiritual is in songs, which are either sentimental or have a kind of general soothing effect.

O'Casey is also adept at conveying *mood* and particularly *tension* through his dialogue, the best instances perhaps being the two outbursts: of Nora, and of Bessie as she lies dying. As with *The Shadow of a Gunman*, the *cockney dialect* spoken by Stoddart and Tinley is a distortion of speech sounds that has a caricature effect. What it does convey, however, is that they too are victims of the situation and can have only certain stereotyped reactions to it: this is admirably captured in their speech.

Characters

In his book, *Sean O'Casey, The Man and His Work*, David Krause says of O'Casey's women that they represent 'his Ireland'; that of 'tenacious mothers and wives' to be found in the tenements he knew so well; 'earthy, shrewd, laughing, suffering, brawling, independent'. And nowhere is this more clearly shown than in *The Plough and the Stars*. Nora, Bessie, Jinny Gogan, Rosie – each has some if not all of the qualities described above; they compare favourably with the men, and earn Krause's definition of them as 'the main heroes'. They are therefore here treated as a group (apart from Rosie).

Nora Clitheroe

She is a young woman of twenty-two, alert, swift, full of nervous energy, and a little anxious to get on in the world.

Nora reflects the reverse side of the coin of patriotism: she is the sufferer, the inevitable victim of her enemy, war; the non-activist who sees all that she has longed for go to ruin, but who struggles hard for her ideal, even until she loses her reason.

We first hear her described by Fluther as 'a pretty little Judy', while Mrs Gogan speaks of her 'upperosity' and 'swank' as well as her rather daring clothes. When she enters we see that she has charm and style, but considerable firmness. She has ambition, first to be a good lover and wife, and second to rise above the tenement way of life (see Mrs Gogan's early comments in Act 1). She also wishes to make her flat a place fit for the baby she is going to have. Her devotion to Jack is intense, matched only by her desire to keep him safe. This is shown by the suppression of the news of his promotion, by her seeking him at the barricades and her later struggle (Act 3) to hold him. He is in her mind at all times; even when she is losing her reason she talks of their walks in the country in happier times, cries out for him, and prattles of his baby.

But Jack, when alive, is not the only object of her concern: family loyalty makes her take in The Covey (Jack's cousin) and Peter

Flynn (her uncle). However, to keep to her ideal of a respectable house, they have to conform; this scandalizes Fluther, for her standards are not in keeping with the true tenement spirit. Her love for Jack does not blind her to his weaknesses. She knows him well enough to realize that he really longs to return to his political activities, which will give him the authority he craves but cannot command.

She is fearful of strife, but shows courage in being different from her censorious neighbours, and real heroism in her frantic search for Jack. She risks the dangers of the streets to find him, and makes her own assault on the barricades, physically and verbally attacking the viragos who represent those who make 'an exhilarating epiphany of the ritual of bloodshed' (Krause).

Her fear, that Jack has the 'coward instinct' that will drive him to leave her for fear of what his comrades will say, is well-founded. She clings to him though he has spoken and acted unkindly ('The agony I'm in since he left me has thrust away every rough thing he done, an' every unkind word he spoke'); when he inevitably deserts her, again roughly and unkindly, she becomes demented. She is, in fact, one of the innocent victims of this small and bloody war, for she is sensitive, self-respecting, true to an ideal – a wish to create something from very little and not, surely, someone to be derided by the Abbey Theatre rioters.

Bessie Burgess

She is a woman of forty, vigorously built. Her face is a dogged one, hardened by toil, and a little coarsened by drink.

She, like Fluther and Mrs Gogan, is old enough (as we see from the above quotation) to have endured much and to have become hardened. Her face, we are told, is at times animated into a scornful and vicious expression; she is a coster-woman, 'a street fruit-vendor', out in all weathers, in perpetual combat with her wholesalers, her customers and the police. No wonder that she tries to forget her troubles by drinking heavily, and no wonder her tongue is a rough one.

She has another problem, or rather two, for she is a Protestant in a mainly Catholic community, and a supporter of King and

Country rather than of Irish patriotism. Her son is a young soldier in the trenches, as she does not cease to remind his neighbours – at the same time talking about those who are safe at home, but though she uses him as a sort of weapon in this way, she worries deeply about him – just as Nora worries about Jack. Like Fluther and Mrs Gogan, Bessie cannot bear to think of any one tenement dweller having ideas of being superior to the rest; hence her animosity to Nora – and to Jack, for she sees him as a sort of social climber in the patriotic movement.

Bessie's speech is rough, though liberally sprinkled with quotations (usually inaccurate) from the scriptures and from hymns: she is a Protestant, probably Presbyterian. She is easily aroused and ready for a quarrel, particularly with her sparring-partner Mrs Gogan; we feel she is cast as a 'holy terror' until we see her unostentatiously comforting Mollser. This tenderness is almost unwilling, and comes from her strength of character and recognition of true need. (Bessie's real goodness is recognized in Act 4 by Mrs Gogan).

These qualities are seen in Bessie's care and concern for Nora, though she is unwilling to take any credit for what she does – indeed she even speaks angrily to her charge, as we see in Act 4 when, after saving Nora's life and being herself mortally wounded, she alternately pleads with Nora for help and reviles her for bringing about her (Bessie's) death. Courageous (she risked her life to get medicine for Mollser); pugnacious; she is another of those whose enemy is war, and who are the unwilling victims of the patriotic ideal. She is an authentic, totally credible, increasingly sympathetic character.

Jinny Gogan

She is a doleful-looking little woman of forty, insinuating manner and sallow complexion. She is fidgety and nervous, terribly talkative.

She is the widow of a man who died in 1915, and was obviously born to be sparring-partner, as we have seen, to Bessie; they even have certain things in common – their widowhood, and the fact that they are both parents. They are also working women, for Jinny is a charwoman, a job which increases her interest in other people's possessions and actions. ('Her heart is aflame with curiosity'.) We see her first in the act of opening Nora's parcel, and we find that she is a sort of living register of all in her district.

She is willing to be more than critical of tenement dwellers who, like Nora, want to rise above their circumstances; perhaps this is a reflection of her own inability to do so. In speech she can be tedious, putting on a sort of balancing act to give the impression that she is really impartial. However, when she is on her favourite subject, Death, she can be quite poetical ('It gives meself a kind o' threspassin' joy to feel meself movin' along in a mournin' coach'), and she excels as a chronicler of fatalities, past and anticipated. She is also a master of the insinuating phrase that hints of slander, and this is a quality she certainly shares with Bessie. And, like her, Jinny has her supporters – and when it comes to a quarrel she can hold her own (see the verbal battles in the bar, Act 2, and those outside the tenement in Act 3). However, she and Bessie become allies in the looting, and return as amiable as may be.

Her attitude to Mollser is casual – she apparently cares about the girl's fears, but is really dismissive of them. It is Bessie who does the real caring, but Jinny realizes this and praises her for it – just as she praises Fluther for his courage. Finally, when Bessie is dead, we see Jinny Gogan taking her place as an organizer: she is destined, as we felt, to be a survivor.

Fluther Good

He is a man of forty years of age, rarely surrendering to thoughts of anxiety, fond of his 'oil' but determined to conquer the habit before he dies.

The detailed and loving description of Fluther and his appearance and characteristics gives the impression that O'Casey has seen, worked with and appreciated men like him. His dress is that of a skilled craftsman of the day (and we see a little later the delight he takes in doing a good job); the seediness of his clothes shows that he is less prosperous than he could be because of his heavy consumption of 'oil' – the whisky that has become a necessity to him. He is aware of his weakness and is bent on giving it up, though he is always ready to relapse. In any argument he usually fills the air with sound and fury. This is proved several times in the course of the play – particularly in his outbursts against The Covey's attacks on The Church and patriotism – and by his nose, broken 'in a fistic battle long ago'. That he enjoys verbal and physical combat is also obvious, when we consider his ready and not always empty threats, and his boasting.

He can, however, be gentle with women, and shows chivalry in his defence of Rosie, even going to the extent of sleeping with her and providing her with spiritual as well as financial comfort. He acts as a peacemaker when the women about him are quarrelling, and only once in the course of the play does he lose his temper with a woman, when he speaks sharply to Mrs Gogan. She has been talking about death, and has aroused in him the fear that he may be ill. This fear is offset by his great courage, shown in his search for Nora and the risk he takes in arranging matters for Mollser's funeral. He is willing to face death too in his looting expedition, which underlines his recklessness, also shown in his defiance of the soldiers (Act 4). He can be a patriot when stirred by the Voice of the Speaker, and is typically eager to prove that he is rather better than Peter where The Cause is concerned. However, he sensibly leaves the declamation of, and fighting for, The Republic to others: as he reminds The Covey, some of his own scars have been gained in fights for the workers' cause.

Fluther is a man of the tenements, interested in his fellows and in the affairs of the moment; shown, for example, by his peering out of the window to see what is going on, though he risks being shot at. Like his fellows he resists misfortune, and determines that life shall go on as near normally as possible (see the games of two-up and cards). Like them, too, he jumps at the chance to snatch some good from misfortune – the motive behind the looting.

Fluther's language gives him, and us, great pleasure. Some may feel that it is not realistic – too vivid and fluent for a carpenter who lives in a slum. Not only does this belittle the working man, it also ignores the fact that 'Dublin English' was the result of a mingling of two adaptable and spirited languages – Elizabethan English and Gaelic. Both these languages are suited to poetry, and each adapts itself to the other, incorporating some of the vocabulary and grammar of each. Fluther's speech is certainly meant to be realistic. Fluther is completely acceptable, a real man, a manifestation of the joy in life that enables us to face its real struggles.

Jack Clitheroe

He is a tall, well-made fellow of twenty-five. His face has none of the strength of Nora's. It is a face in which is the desire for authority, without the power to attain it.

Krause speaks also of O'Casey's men, some of whom are 'frustrated and gulled by dreams', which they cannot 'convert into realities'; Clitheroe is one such. He should, to satisfy the patriotic Irishmen of 1926, have been the hero of the play; in fact he definitely plays second fiddle to the women; even the trio Fluther. The Covey and Peter Flynn upstage him. If we bear in mind the extract under his name, above, we shall see how true it is in the light of the unfolding action of the play.

When we first see Jack he is a devoted husband, a bricklayer with the money to provide for his wife and the willingness to help her in her ambition to improve their position. He has even given up the Irish Citizen Army – mainly, however, because he has been disappointed in his quest for promotion. His heart is still with the Army, and this makes him snap at Nora when she twits him about it. Then, when Brennan arrives and Clitheroe finds that she has burned his letter of appointment to the rank of Commandant, exasperation turns to anger, and he treats her roughly, rushing off to a meeting with the hint that he may not return. Here we see him exerting the sort of authority that is easily called into use against the physically weak and the spiritually vulnerable.

At the meeting Jack is fired by the rhetoric of the speaker, which inspires him to fight for an ideal of a republic (though he should have been, as The Covey realizes, fighting in the cause of the workers). How bitterly he regrets this cause is shown in Act 3. War is not what he had expected, and he longs to be with his wife. Clitheroe still has his basic decency, for he refuses to fire on the people who are shouting and jeering, realizing they are Irishmen and brothers, and not the 'lice' Brennan calls them.

We recognize the truth in Nora's remark, that fear is taking him away from her again – fear of being called a coward, of not conforming. We deplore the violence Jack again uses against her; but we cannot help seeing that he does owe a duty to a terribly wounded companion, and that he is morally bound to try to finish the job he has started. This he does, unlike Brennan, and he should qualify for the role of hero and martyr, but there is no doubt that, through the flaws in his character, he brought about his own destruction.

The Covey

He is about twenty-five, tall, thin ... Heavy seams fall from each side of his nose, down around his lips, as if they were suspenders keeping his mouth from falling.

We only know him by this name, except that Nora once calls him Willie; the nickname carries with it 'wide-boy' associations, fitting in with his 'education' and skill in argument. He is a skilled man – a fitter – and like many of his class, has 'red' tendencies. His patriotism is for his own class, and he has a working-class intellectual's ideas of science and Darwinism. He propounds these theories in a slow wailing drawl, rather as some intellectuals do today. He takes a poor view of the Church; this disgusts Fluther, who wants it kept out of everything. He also resents nationalism, because it presents an out-of-date and possibly mistaken ideal, which is basically opposed to the socialism by which he lives. His 'Bible' is Jenersky – he is shocked when Peter titters while he reads it, and he offers the book with missionary zeal to Rosie and Corporal Stoddart.

The Covey takes a delight in goading Peter; he likes to promote arguments, rises to them, and is in fact a stirrer up of trouble – though he is quick to retreat when attacked. His fear extends to Rosie, and he abuses her roundly. When challenged by Fluther he behaves out of character (or is he pretending?) and squares up to Fluther – or would do so were he not being held. However, he knuckles under to Nora. He has, despite his often averred principles, an eye for the main chance; he looks for loot, and risks his life to get it. And his main concern – apart from his Socialistic creed – is self-preservation.

Peter Flynn

His face wears an expression of animated anguish, mixed with irritated defiance, as if everybody was at war with him, and he with everybody.

He is a labourer, hence somewhat despised and teased by the skilled men, towards whom he displays some awkwardness, and with whom he sometimes quarrels. His deadliest enemy is The Covey, for the latter despises nationalism and taunts him with quotations from Moore's Irish songs. In fact everyone can be Peter's enemy, for he bristles when he thinks someone is belittling him, and abuses them freely, thus giving an impression of insecurity. His devotion to The Cause and the Foresters seems to be an attempt to give himself an identity – even some authority. Peter considers himself to be the patriot par excellence because of his yearly visits to Bodenstown, and he is roused to frenzy and fervour by the voice of the Speaker. He can be moved to take action against detractors (rushes at The Covey with a sword, though he won't use it) and is very free with abuse. In reality he is anxious if not cowardly, trying to avoid the pub argument and dithering about looting (prudence wins), and he exerts himself to keep Fluther away from the window. Perhaps this is due in part to his age; he might even have welcomed action when he was younger. He is a natural supporter of trouble and another one who enjoys stirring things up. Probably he will take the view that his rounding-up by the Army is almost equivalent to imprisonment, which he will be able to boast about when the time comes. He seems to be symbolic of those who encourage and ferment, but don't actually take part; thus any risks he runs are incidental, not foreseen. He stands, too, for the purely selfish or egocentric man, but strangely – as with Jinny Gogan and Fluther – his speech can reach poetic heights when he is in a state of fury.

Minor characters

Captain Brennan is the representative of the membership of the Irish Citizen Army, though he is not the average working man; after all, he had his own business. It is easy to imagine that he may, like Clitheroe, have wanted authority, or to be 'in the swim' – one feels that he would have liked to be in the more socially acceptable Irish Volunteers. At first he is seen only as a man in a uniform, spouting pseudo-military jargon, and we hear him referred to as a 'bit of a thick' who had been 'sweet on' Nora. Later he develops into a man filled with the idea of being a liberator of the people (who may not want his sort of liberation). Hardened by his trade of killing and selling chickens, he wants to shoot down the 'slum lice' who are mocking him. However, he has had enough decency to try to protect Nora from Jack Clitheroe's anger, though in Act 3 he appears to have lost all sympathy with her, urging Jack to 'break her hold' and leave her. In fact by Act 3 he seems to have lost some of his own fervour, though there is some sense in his having changed out of his uniform into civilian clothes. Moreover, he is telling the truth (when charged with leaving the dead Clitheroe behind), when he replies, 'I took me chance as well as him.' Certainly, though he proves that discretion is the better part of valour, he *has* valour.

We do not know whether Brennan was released from imprisonment (or even if he was imprisoned) but if so, he was certainly of the type to be marked out for a government job in the new republic; he may even have been one of the mob that rioted against O'Casey's play when it was presented at the Abbey Theatre in 1926.

Like Brennan, *Lieutenant Langon* is not described in any detail in the stage directions. All we know of him is that he is a civil servant, and one of the Irish volunteers. Thus we can gather that he is one of the 'boorzwawzee' with a privileged position in some government office, and the fashionable desire to be an Irish patriot. He is easily mesmerized by the words of the Man at the Window, and does not realize what war involves – as we see when he says 'Ireland is greater than a mother' and craves for 'Wounds for the Independence of Ireland'. He may well have been like the men Nora saw at the barricade, men with fear in their eyes, who shot at other men who felt the same fear of death and who were also to become 'inevitable casualties' – the born losers of any war.

Rosie Redmond is a prostitute, and when the audience at the Abbey Theatre rioted during the performance of *The Plough* in 1926, some of their anger was directed at the suggestion that Irish girls could belong to the oldest profession; but they must have known that prostitutes had been a feature of Dublin life for a very long time. Rosie was one such, who lived in the Digs: tolerated, if not licensed brothels, where she was charged for board, laundry, with an extra rental charge for every customer she took home. If the barman can be a father confessor at times, she can be a sort of temple prostitute, confided in by her customers, and doing a useful service (though possibly at their own risk) for single or unhappily married men needing a natural outlet for their appetites and frustrated affections.

In a different sense, Rosie is like Bessie, in that she plies her trade in the streets. Well-built and pretty and, given the chance, she can be a good companion. Even when she is trying to drum up trade it is mainly to improve her dress and condition; in a more conventional occupation, such ambition would be laudable. She is tolerated, perhaps liked, but not trusted by the bartender, and her trade is easily recognizable. She will put up with a certain amount of roughish word-play, but has her feelings, and is upset by The Covey. However, she is comforted by the chivalrous Fluther, and goes out with him singing a gay little air which, like her, is a manifestation of the spirit of creative life. Angry critics may perhaps have objected to the fact that O'Casey obviously preferred her to the dour or rabid patriots.

Other minor characters include *Corporal Stoddart* and *Sergeant Tinley*. Their ranks, and their reference to a 'dawg-foight', lead us to believe that they are men who have had experience at the front: they may even have been wounded there and are perhaps briefly posted on home service. To them 'the country' is the entire United Kingdom; and Stoddart the Socialist has put aside his political creed so that he may preach it safely in time of peace. Their tolerance of, and rough kindness to, the people of the tenement is balanced by their contempt and hatred of the 'enemy', who lurks behind the windows of the houses, snipes at them, and uses dum-dum bullets. Thus they are expressing the views of the average British soldier (Bessie's son might have felt the same). O'Casey must have known many like them: that is why he cannot bang the Fenian drum and make them villains.

The woman. Her comments, like those of the soldiers, add to the picture of what is going on in the streets. Distressed and uncomprehending, she serves as an example to prove that the middle classes as well as the poor can suffer from war.

Mollser is the poor girl who is a typical victim of the slums – she is what any fighting should be about. Consumptive, she is neglected by her mother – who is driven to impatience with her because she is a useless mouth, and takes up time that can ill be spared from the battle for living. She is a statistic for The Covey and for O'Casey, a symbol of what is truly wrong with Ireland. No wonder she is impatient with her mother when asked about her health (which both know is failing); no wonder she looks again for anybody with a 'titther of sense'.

The *bartender* is one of the men of power in the slums of Dublin. He is both servant and master, selling the release his customers want, but able to withhold it if they have no money, infringe 'the rules of the house', or upset his ideas of decorum. He has some tolerance, and is willing to change his manner to suit the customer of the moment – though eager to appear impartial. He is a magisterial character, regarded by some with as much reverence as a priest would merit.

The Figure in the Window (whose words are attributed to the Voice of the Man) plays no part in the action before or after Act 2. He therefore cannot be considered as a character (though O'Casey would have known him if the voice had been that of Patrick Pearse). The Figure and the words represent a force that is stirring men to action; glorifying the idea of war for a cause; paying reverence to the idea of blood shed in sacrifice; praising 'the exhilaration of war' – all this after two years of terrible conflict, clearly reported. And the words stir the listeners into rushing to offer themselves as the blood-sacrifice that is being called for.

Act summaries and textual notes

Note to the student

Spelling and pronunciation Since the dialogue in this play contains much phonetic spelling, to avoid tedious, unnecessary repetition of notes we give a few hints on pronunciation and spelling. 'dh' and 'th' as in 'slander' and 'water' are a consequence of Gaelic forms being imposed upon English words; the hard 'd' is softened, almost to equal 'th' as in 'thou', and the hard 't' is converted, almost to equal 'th' in 'thorough'.
The broad 'i' of 'thigh' and 'eye' becomes 'oi'.
The 'e' of 'Jesus' becomes 'ay' as in 'say'. Occasionally the 'h' which would normally follow a 't' is omitted – so we have Peter's favourite 'twarted' instead of 'thwarted'.
Unusual grammatical constructions are noted as they occur.

Currency The pound (or sovereign) in 1916 was divided into twenty shillings, which were subdivided into twelve pence, twenty-four half-pence or forty-eight farthings. Other coins were the sixpenny piece (or 'tanner'), the shilling which was called a 'bob', the three-penny piece or 'joey', the florin or 'two-bob' (two-shilling piece), and the half-crown ('half-dollar') which was worth two shillings and sixpence. The crown (five shillings) was not often seen, and the guinea (one pound and one shilling) was a notional unit of currency. It is pointless to express all this in today's currency, as the pound has deteriorated so much in value in the last sixty-odd years.

Title and dedication

Title

This is taken from the device on the banner of the Irish Transport and General Workers' Union and their Citizen Army. The back-ground of the banner was blue, and O'Casey's description, in his *Autobiography* (Pan Books), indicates 'the formalised shape of a plough, a golden-brown colour, seamed with a rusty red', while through all glittered 'the stars of the Plough ... The plough will always be there to furrow the earth, the stars will always be there to unveil the beauty of the night, and a newer people, leading a newer life, will sing like the sons of the morning.'

Dedication

'To the gay laugh of my mother at the gate of the grave.' While her son was out she rose from her deathbed to do the washing, and joked with the neighbours while she hung it out.

Act 1

'In rooms of gilded splendour ... the poor languished from hunger, disease and cold.' So writes Ulick O'Connor in *Oliver St John Gogarty and his Times* (Cape), and in one such place three of the four acts in *The Plough and the Stars* are set. It was typical – a town-house built in the eighteenth century for a rich landowner, who later left it to be bought by a slum landlord. It was then divided into one- and two-room flats, which the owner let to the poor – having first removed everything that was saleable, even to the marble fireplaces. The house teemed with people from attic to basement; in 1913 one such house was reported to contain 107 dwellers, while another had one lavatory for 70 people. In that year Dublin's death-rate was the highest in Europe, most of the deaths being caused by tuberculosis and other respiratory diseases. People sought relief in drink, and in the kind of 'commodious public-house' of Act 2.

The first stage direction in Act 1 shows in some detail how a self-respecting and ambitious tenant has made a great effort to create a decent home – unusually large since it has two rooms, though these have to accommodate four tenants. One of the tenants, Peter Flynn, is pottering about dressing himself for an important event, and is annoyed by the presence of a carpenter, Fluther Good. Each is described in some detail.

Neither is speaking, and the most noticeable sound is coming from the street, where a gang of labourers is repairing the roadway.

Then Mrs Gogan's voice is heard off-stage. She is speaking to a messenger from a dress shop, and is taking delivery of a parcel for Mrs Clitheroe, wife of the chief tenant of the flat. Once inside again, she behaves as one would expect from the author's description. She opens the parcel, and begins a commentary on Mrs Clitheroe – and her wishes to make the place respectable and rise above the normal life of the tenement, while the way she dresses and her attitudes towards the two sub-tenants and her husband are described. (The Covey and Peter Flynn are the sub-tenants.) Jinny Gogan establishes herself as a comic character by her manner of speaking: a relentless stream, interrupted occasionally by a well-turned phrase.

The responses of her companions show that there is to be a meeting that evening of the supporters of the as yet non-existent republic of Ireland; that Peter is attending in his uniform; that Fluther is indifferent to the cause; and that Jack Clitheroe will also not be attending, much to the delight of his wife. Her relief arises from the fact that he has resigned from the Irish Citizen Army – partly, the gossips say, because he has not been given the promotion he thought he deserved.

After the feather-headed, basically spiteful, Mrs Gogan has driven Fluther into a rage by talking about illness and death (of which he has a superstitious fear), the unseen workers down tools and march off, cheering, to prepare for the evening's demonstration. Almost immediately The Covey enters, annoyed because he believes nationalism to be irrelevant. He claims that human beings, considered generally, are more important than patriots, and takes the opportunity to enlarge on the scientist's view of man's origin and functions, as opposed to that of the Church. He thus succeeds in annoying Peter and Fluther – no difficult task, especially as he has a long-standing feud with the former. Finally goaded to the limit, Peter makes for him with his sword, and The Covey rushes through the door, then continues to talk through the keyhole.

He is interrupted by Nora, whose appearance, speech and actions confirm the belief of Mrs Gogan and others that she is longing to improve her condition and her station in life. In the dialogue that follows we have confirmation, too, that Fluther is trying to become a teetotaller (though one feels he overdoes his protestations), and that The Covey's chief interest is in the proletariat. Bessie Burgess, a heavy drinker herself, enters. In violent language, with Biblical echoes, she makes an attack on Nora; she stops when Jack Clitheroe enters and hustles her out.

The semblance of a respectable family meal follows, attended by Peter in the uniform of an Irish National Forester, but peace is soon destroyed by The Covey, who quarrels with the old man and denounces the Irish Citizen Army for supporting the cause of the Nationalists rather than the workers. Clitheroe's resentment against the Citizen Army shows his jealousy of Captain Brennan, but after the others have been hustled off he and Nora are pleasant together, in fact romantic – until there is a knock on the door.

At the sound of a voice asking for 'Commandant Clitheroe' Nora shows signs of agitation, but her husband quietens her and admits Brennan, who is in the full uniform of a Captain in the Irish Citizen Army. He gives Clitheroe his orders to parade, and when Clitheroe shows surprise (particularly at being addressed as 'Commandant'), points out that a message had previously been delivered to Nora. She after trying to persuade her husband not to go, admits that she has burned the letter; she is assailed physically and vocally by Clitheroe, whose first use of the authority he has always longed for is aimed at his wife.

As Nora sits, disconsolate, she is approached by Mollser, Mrs Gogan's daughter who is dying of consumption. Mollser is a victim of poverty and disease, and her appearance is described briefly but with harrowing effect. She has come to seek company to allay her fear of death. Before she has finished speaking, the sound of military music is heard; the band is playing the Dublin Fusiliers to the docks, and they are singing what O'Casey describes in his *Autobiography* as a sort of second national anthem – 'It's a long way to Tipperary'. These troops are on the way to France. As Mollser and Nora sit listening, Bessie (who has already said that her son is at the Front) makes a bitter comment from the doorway on those who prosper at home while others are killed overseas. Her speech again carries biblical undertones, and it ends prophetically.

The theme of this act is conflict – domestic and comic (Peter and The Covey, Fluther and Mrs Gogan, Fluther and The Covey);

soon to become tragic (Jack and Nora Clitheroe). There is also Nora's lonely battle for respectability and self-respect in the face of the bitter comments of those (particularly Mrs Gogan and Bessie) who do not wish her to rise above her station. Mollser is struggling against death and her fear of it; Clitheroe and Brennan are preparing to fight for Irish independence. These smaller conflicts are set against the huge backcloth of the Great War, which transcends all the rest.

back drawing-room In this part of the room, separated from the front by folding doors, the musical part of an evening's entertainment was given.
a calendar ... 'The Sleeping Venus' There was not just one picture with this subject, so it is difficult to say who the painter was. (It must have been a large calendar if the audience could see it.)
casement-cloth A lightweight, very often handsome material used (as its name suggests) for curtains; sometimes 'arty' ladies would make dresses of it.
Robert Emmet See note p.30.
'The Gleaners' ... 'The Angelus' Popular prints of paintings by Millet, who specialized in pictures of peasants.
delf ware Originally made (mainly in blue and white) at Delft in Holland, a kind of glazed, strong china-ware.
gate-legged table With legs in a frame, swinging back to allow the leaves to be shut down.
gasolene lamp Probably O'Casey means a 'paraffin lamp', since it is a temporary light for workmen repairing the street outside.
oil (slang) Drink.
seedy Shabby.
jerry hat A bowler-hat (from its shape).
sound and fury A Shakespearian echo from *Macbeth* (Act V, Scene 5, lines 27–8).
lozenge Like a conventional diamond – broad at the cheekbones, tapering away to brow and chin.
singlet Sleeveless vest.
Arnott's A well-known dressmaker's and tailor's store. (The Citizen Army had its first fifty uniforms made there at a cost of £1 each.)
upperosity Snobbishness – wanting to rise 'above her position'.
Judy Slang for 'girl'.
glad-neck A low-cut, provocative neckline.

two turtle doves A popular symbol for romantic affection.
just been afther Just then been.
derogatory Fluther uses the word here in its proper sense – 'condemnatory' – but it is a pet word of his, often misused: it is a good exercise to work out what he means every time he uses it!
foostherin' Fussing.
fealty Loyalty.
th' Irish Republic Non-existent at that time.
Parnell Square The unfashionable end of O'Connell Street.
up th' pole 'On the wagon' – not taking alcoholic drink.
canonicals His uniform, she means, but to him the 'cause' is a religion.
best Get the upper hand of.
Citizen Army See section on 'Background'.
th' Red Hand o' Liberty Hall The badge of the ICA.
a Sam Browne belt So named after the British Officer who invented it: a leather waist-belt and cross-strap over one or both shoulders (at that time).
put out th' street-lamps on him He displayed it until the lamp-man turned off the gas lamp (admirable thrift!).
herself i.e. Mrs Clitheroe.
figaries She means filigree decoration.
it's a baby's rattle Fluther is jeering at the old man's fear of death – but as we see a little later he too is a bit of a coward.
get his goat i.e. annoy him.
has a few jars up i.e. has had a few beers.
You'd want to be careful We are introduced for the first time to Mrs Gogan's obsessive interest in sickness and death. Her lack of interest – through ignorance – in her own daughter's condition is one of the tragic ironies of the play.
threspassin' Sinful.
Lord Mayor's nightdhress Large, white, frilled – Peter's shirt must be suitable for that notable (whose beautiful Mansion House is one of the splendid features of Dublin).
fermentin' Boiling over.
dizzy as bedamned i.e. as dizzy as can be.
political baptisimal vows He makes the comparison (patriotism and religion) that Mrs Gogan has made when talking of Peter.
in seculo seculorum For 'e' read 'ae' – for ages and ages.
mollycewels i.e. molecules.
cunundrhums i.e. conundrums, riddles.
manifestin' forth Proof of.

twart Thwart.

th' man o' Java The remains, found in that island, of a remote ancestor of man.

tap your rubbidge o' thoughts Pour out your rubbishy ideas.

leppin' Leaping.

word-weavin' little ignorant yahoo The Covey certainly has a vocabulary, though it is doubtful if he could be called a 'yahoo' (a brutish or degraded creature), which is from *Gulliver's Travels* by Jonathan Swift – another Dublin man.

a prime lassie i.e. a somewhat immoral young woman.

aself i.e. even if you *are* Nora's pet.

I'll leave you to th' day A wonderful confusion of God and the angels and their functions with those of the devil and his imps.

animosities i.e. belittling remarks.

Dear harp o' me counthry From Thomas Moore's *Irish Melodies*.

a free pass i.e. an invitation.

th' hardy habit A good, self-respecting habit.

inaugurate th' customs i.e. behave like the other (disreputable) tenants in my rooms.

flit Move.

bowsey Drunken.

'ill Will.

meet . . . with an encore i.e. get as good as you give.

a door of a select bar A typical simile of a haunter of public houses.

You're a whole man i.e. a fine fellow and a good tradesman.

as much chance A fine simile; what could be more deaf than a dead man?

has a few up i.e. is tipsy.

throllop i.e. trollop, whore.

bargin' Abusing – from the idea that barge-men were supposed to be profane.

out of her i.e. out of her mouth.

g'up ower Go upstairs, out of this room.

guzzle Throttle.

he'd see me righted He'd stand up for me.

sorra fear Never a chance.

Foresters The Irish National Foresters: a sort of patriotic friendly society, the southern equivalent of an Orange lodge.

assed Asked.

a bit of a thick Rather stupid.

Because it's a Labour flag Fairly representative of the views of the Irish TGWU.

Your mind is th' mind of a mummy i.e. dead and carefully preserved.

Oh, where's the slave so lowly From Thomas Moore's *Irish Melodies*.

varmint i.e. vermin.

the illegitimate son What could be worse, he thinks, than the bastard of a bastard whose father had a minor rank in an army of 'greasers' or 'dagoes'.

Now, your hat's on, your house is thatched A real country expression, usually said to children.

snotty Slang – indignant in an unpleasant way.

Bridlin' up i.e. rearing up.

You take a body up too quickly i.e. you pick up what I am saying too sharply.

When you and I were young, Maggie A popular drawing-room ballad, suitable for an Irish tenor.

General Jim Connolly Leader of the Citizen Army, executed after the Easter Rising (see 'Background').

Commandant Leader of a battalion; in the British Army at this time this position was sometimes filled by a Major, often by a Lieutenant-Colonel. A battalion would be a very small unit.

a reconnaissance attack A 'fake' attack. (There were many of these made: the police turned a blind eye because the authorities did not want to 'create disturbances'.)

I burned it She is driven to anger by his sudden return of interest in the ICA (and his promotion), and he retaliates – typically – by hurting her.

I don't care if you never come back But she later shows just how much she does care for him.

It's a long way to Tipperary This is still popular as a marching song of the British Army. (A nice foil to Brennan's whistling of 'The Soldiers' Song'.)

There's th' men marchin' out Bessie thinks of the Fusiliers going to fight the Germans, and of her son already in the trenches. She contrasts them with those staying at home (though the ones in her house can hardly be thought of as 'feedin' on the fatness o' the land'). She continues with a confused sense of biblical phrasing.

Act 2

The setting is the bar of a public house in Parnell Square, at the unfashionable end of O'Connell Street. The description of the interior is detailed and interested.

The two occupants of the bar are devoted servants of the Dublin public – the barman and Rosie Redmond. The latter is a prostitute, good-looking, and dressed as well as her means permit; she is bemoaning the poor state of her trade. The barman speaks of the great meeting – four platforms are in use – and they interrupt their conversation to listen to the speaker praising the ideal of the blood sacrifice. (He sounds like, and may well be intended to be, Padraic Pearse). When he speaks of 'things more horrible than bloodshed' Rosie heartily agrees – and one feels that she thinks the loss of her trade may be one of the 'horrible' things. The barman predictably says that he would be there but for his age – an easy sort of patriotism which has some echo in the words of Peter and Fluther, who have just entered. The speaker's words have set them afire, and they want to stoke up with liquid fuel. Each tries to outdo the other in expressing his feelings; but Fluther has the edge, for his speech is more high-flown, even if he does fall into his characteristic malapropisms.

They pause to listen to the speaker, who this time speaks in glowing terms of the Great War as a blood-sacrifice, and inspires such ardour in the two (who only imagine themselves as revolutionary heroes) that they rush out again to listen more closely. They pass The Covey on his way in, and he, apparently taken aback by the sight of Peter strutting arrogantly, calls for a whisky. Rosie, scenting a prosperous and profitable customer, approaches and immediately appropriates his drink. Clumsily he tries to avoid her, and begins his usual proletarian line of speech, but she pays no heed and tries to force herself on him; he flees, frightened of her.

Yet again the two would-be heroes enter, this time accompanied by Mrs Gogan, who is carrying a baby which she later soothes by dipping her finger in whisky and putting it in its mouth – a pacifier well known to generations of slum mothers. By now drink has inflamed rather than pacified Fluther; he tries to pick a quarrel with Peter over the latter's claim to be a patriot of long standing, and just as Mrs Gogan is soothing the two men, The Covey enters with Bessie Burgess, who immediately begins 'talking at' the other group, while apparently talking to her companion. There is a brief silence while they listen again to the speaker, who claims that Ireland 'must welcome' war – which is somewhat ironical when one considers the hundreds of Irishmen already in the trenches, and that (as she has already said) Bessie's son is one of them.

The argument (a small war in itself) between the two women intensifies, and in spite of the efforts of Peter and Fluther to calm things down, they square up to each other. Peter, at first pushed out of the way by Bessie, is handed the baby by Mrs Gogan, so that she can get on with the battle. The scene becomes comic when the barman throws the two women out, and Peter is left literally 'holding the baby'. He tries to call the mother back, and to involve The Covey and Fluther in his efforts to get rid of the child; in the end he has to go out, carrying it, in search of its mother.

Now Rosie, who has obviously slipped out in quest of trade, returns and tries to scrounge a drink from the barman. He refuses, but Fluther stands her one, saying that the meeting will soon be over (and, by implication, that her 'trade' will improve). When The Covey remarks that what has been said is all nonsense, Fluther naturally disagrees and, on being told that talk of Irish patriotism is 'dope for the Boorzwawzee' (bourgeoisie), angrily shows the scars he has received in battles for the proletariat. The Covey continues to talk of the labour movement in terms of economic Marxism, which Fluther cannot understand. Rosie intervenes with a slighting remark about The Covey, who twits her with being a prostitute: Fluther comes to the aid of the angry humiliated girl, threatening to 'beat up' his companion. The two men, with much 'sound and fury', go into the classic 'hold me back' routine. They are separated by the barman, who evicts The Covey, leaving Fluther and Rosie to comfort each other in the snug: a small private bar for intimate meetings.

Three men now enter: Commandant Clitheroe and Captain Brennan of the Irish Citizen Army, and Lieutenant Langon of the Irish Volunteers. Predictably (for they are now members of the Officer class) they call for port, as it is a 'refined' drink. They begin breathing fire, which is stirred by the words of the speaker, who is now rousing hatred by calling the crowd to remember their dead Fenian heroes. Snatching up the banners, they toast the future that awaits them when they fight for their cause: imprisonment, wounds, death. Langon's mother and Clitheroe's wife are as nothing compared with the cause of Ireland's liberty; at the sound of the bugle they rush out. Their place is taken by Rosie and Fluther – he a little drunk (but not incapable) and she happy in the knowledge that she has got him. Outside is heard the voice of an officer ordering the Irish Volunteers to march off. This is followed by a similar order to the Irish Citizen Army; but Rosie and Fluther march off in irregular order, to the tune of a lively, bawdy little song from the girl.

Again the themes are those of conflict. Peter and Fluther quarrel because Peter thinks that Fluther is claiming to be a better patriot than he. Fluther wants to fight The Covey, mainly over the question of patriotism versus proletarianism. Rosie is battling for a living and perhaps the cause of love (commercial though it may be). Bessie and Mrs Gogan are engaged in a battle of words – almost of blows – which involves an assault by each on the other's character. The Speaker calls for a bloody battle in Ireland to match the great conflict outside, and the three young men pledge themselves to the forthcoming battle.

commodious i.e. spacious.

carafe Wide-mouthed bottle for water (or wine).

snug 'Private' bar.

half of whisky In England, a small or single whisky.

in a wine-glass To make it look more refined.

Curse o' God on th' haporth God damn the little I've earned.

pretty petticoat Pretty girl.

dials Faces.

You'd think ... a girl's garthers Solemn dedicated patriots, ready to die for the cause but with no eyes for a pretty, well-displayed and well-decorated leg.

spoutin' out of him Same form as 'bargin' out' in Act 1; 'spouting' is slang for 'orating'.

oil Whisky.

th' grave of Wolfe Tone See note pp.35 and 63.

Get th' Dublin men Local patriotism, the capital as against the provinces.

slim thinkin' Shrewd, cunning.

compromization The merest hint of being involved in action.
leppin' Jumping.
The blood was BOILIN' Bombastic metaphor – perhaps half true.
blatherin' Incessant chat.
The old heart of the earth The blood-sacrifice theme of Patrick (Padraic) Pearse.
a glass o' malt A full measure (in England a 'double') of whisky.
th' young gentleman's ordherin' it I can tell he means to buy me a drink.
What are you houldin' on out o' you for Again, the familiar construction – 'Why are you saying "Hold on"?'
bird Girl.
Jiggs A cartoon character, widely syndicated in a national newspaper before the war.
a flash in th' pan i.e. temporary.
Look here, comrade . . . Jenersky's Again the inevitable pamphlet. But Rosie goes into action.
exemplified glad neck Exactly what a low-cut dress should be – a fine specimen of a plunging neckline. But she scares The Covey.
ass i.e. ask.
bridie Bride.
shinannickin' afther Judies i.e. making passes at girls.
a mot Slang for 'a girl', usually used in a disreputable sense.
tittle i.e. tickle.
a lassie like you Again the word is used in a truly 'derogatory' sense.
Jasus, it's in a monasthery A fine piece of lively vernacular speech.
spendin' our holidays Going into a retreat.
our adorers i.e. knees in the position of prayer.
tellin' our beads Counting off the prayers on our rosaries.
buzzums Bosoms.
It's my rule Peter is imitating Fluther, who is boiling up for a quarrel with somebody.
When yous are goin' along A nice vision of death, rather like the one to which she treated Fluther in Act 1.
Bodenstown Twelve miles from Dublin, and the site of the grave or memorial to Wolfe Tone.
scabbin' it on th' clergy Doing the job of the priests.
aroree boree allis Aurora Borealis: the Northern Lights.
I always think th' kilts is hardly decent Remember that a good many Gaelic Irishmen wore the kilt.

asy Easy, quietly.
poor little Catholic Belgium This is taken from the recruiting posters specially designed for Catholic Irishmen.
stupefy i.e. stop your foolishness (by getting drunk).
Tommies British soldiers; from 'Thomas Atkins', one of the names given in King's Regulations to the culprit in a military trial.
Whisht Hush.
dip our thoughts A long-winded way of saying 'a woman whom sensible people can't understand'.
bevy Group, bunch.
flappers A 1920s word for frivolous young women, dedicated to the social whirl.
whose feet abideth not i.e. who doesn't stay.
green-accoutred figures A slighting reference to Peter's appearance in his Forester's uniform.
over at th' other end of th' shop i.e. from his end of the bar.
dipping her fingers in the whisky That, or gin, made the classic pacifier of babies for shiftless or desperate women.
Dope, dope! An adaptation of 'religion is the opium (opiate?) of the people.
Saint Vincent de Paul man This refers to a charitable society which made cash allowances to the poor; the latter were supposed to use the money for necessities, and visitors were sent out to check that this was done.
packin' up knowledge accordin' to her conscience Such knowledge as she possesses has been gained by conscientious thought.
precept upon precept Refers to Isaiah, 28,10.
weddin' lines Marriage certificate. This is a nasty reference to the young baby, but Mrs Gogan's words show that her husband had died in 1915 while she was already carrying his child.
An' that's more than some o' you can say She is always ready with a piece of oratory: she means that Bessie only pretends to be virtuous, and is easily tempted: but this is not true, either.
wizenin' up your soul Shrivelling or drying it up. Both women are now well away, slandering each other, but it's entertaining to hear them, except for the barman, who wants no quarrelling.
bum Tramp, beggar.
ever Every.
I don't want to have another endorsement He has a well-kept pub, but his customers sometimes get him into trouble with the law because of their behaviour.

I'll run out in front o' God Almighty Keep on jeering at me and I'll break God's law and kill you.
thrim Trim.
chiselur Child.
Shan Van Vok A symbolic character of Ireland in distress. (Properly 'Shan Van Vocht'.)
Boorzwawzee Bourgeoisie – middle classes – a contemptuous reference.
A skelp from a bobby's baton A blow from a policeman's truncheon.
Phoenix Park A large, rather beautiful park, containing the Viceroy's lodge and the Wellington Memorial.
chancers Liars.
Karl Marx (1818–83); the founder of Marxism, from which Communism is derived.
prate Idle chatter.
I have you well taped I have you sized up.
puss Mouth.
a fair hunt A good chance of being well treated.
Mary o' th' Curlin' Hair He is referring to Rosie.
a Christianable consthruction i.e. you'll look at things like a Christian.
lowser Low character.
some snots flyin' around i.e. I'll punch your nose.
malignified Insulted and abused.
he's fallin' yet A boastful remark about his power.
rotten ripe The fruit (time) is so ripe that it is about to fall, and bring in the era of revolution.
our Fenian dead Irish revolutionaries fallen in battle.
Assembly The British Army called it 'The Fall-in'.
Are you goin' to come home 'To my place', she means.
I once had a lover The verses are probably O'Casey's.

Act 3

The time is Easter Monday 1916; the rebellion has started. There is again a detailed description of the slum tenement. Mrs Gogan is settling her child in the sunshine and asks her how she feels, but we feel that she is not really much interested, since her reassurances are perfunctory. In any case, she is not doing much to calm the girl's fears, for she starts talking about death – at first of Clitheroe (a genuine foreboding, or an inspired guess?). She is interrupted by The Covey and Peter, who seem to have formed a strange alliance; their conversation – interrupted only by Mrs Gogan's account of her vision of Nora's death – gives an outline of the events of the day so far (see 'Background').

From the window of her room Bessie shouts her scorn of the rebels (remember she has a son in the trenches in France). But Mrs Gogan tells the others to pay no heed, and enlarges on her vision of Fluther's death. She stops when he appears with Nora, thus disappointing her expectations. However, she bears up bravely and comforts Nora, who tells of her search for Jack and how she has been derided by the men at the barricades (for putting herself before 'the cause') and by a woman (probably Countess Markiewicz or one of her associates) whom she has attacked physically while cursing the rebels. She, at least, is not one of those who, according to Bessie, have been 'kissin' an' cuddlin' their boys into th' sheddin' of blood'.

Nora confirms that she was thinking only of her husband and their marriage, and tells of the fear in the eyes of the men, and of their laughter; and of the contorted body of the dead man. Thus we see, on a small scale, the image of what was happening every day at the front. We are not prepared, however, to see Mrs Gogan in the role of comforter; after all, she was censorious enough in Act 1, and has been rather perfunctory in her attentions to her own daughter.

As Bessie moves, silent and scornful, into the street, Peter and Fluther begin a game of two-up, with The Covey as the tosser; they are briefly interrupted when they hear the sound of artillery. (This gives us the opportunity to see the fire-eating Peter as 'prudent' if not actually cowardly – rather as he appeared towards the end of Act 2.) The game is resumed and Bessie appears with an odd variety of loot, and tells of the people breaking into and plundering the shops: a vivid description of how looters will behave without logic or forethought. The men decide to join in, but Peter is too fearful, and The Covey and Fluther are jeering at him when a fashionably dressed woman enters [O'Casey gives her a travesty of middle-class speech]; she asks her way to the suburb of Wrathmines (usually spelt without the 'W') but the men, anxious for loot or just fearful, refuse to help her.

When the woman leaves, Mrs Gogan enters, pushing a pram which becomes the subject of a violent outburst when Bessie disputes her right to it; however, they go off together to join the looters. Peter thinks of following them (they will make two stout protectors – or at least stop some bullets), but changes his mind when the big gun fires again. He is joined by The Covey, who is carrying a sack of flour and a ham, and the two start one of their interminable quarrels, with Peter talking smugly about those who revile the sacrifices of 'the boys'. The two women re-enter, their pram laden with an odd assortment of plunder, mainly clothing; they are chatting quite amicably, such is the unifying influence of good work shared, and are not too happy to be interrupted by Peter. He tells Mrs Gogan, to her annoyance, that Mollser is ill and that the baby has convulsions. A rifle shot is heard, and the two women rush inside as Brennan, Clitheroe and Langon, who is wounded, come in (Langon has been granted the wish he voiced in Act 2). Their first words tell of the attitude of the slum-dwellers who were 'mobbin' the men ... risking their lives for them'.

Nora now rushes from the house, and the main part of the action is concerned with her agonized appeal to Clitheroe to stay with her, and with his reactions to her desperate words. He is ashamed of her having gone to the barricades, and will not consent to stay: partly from a quite proper sense that he must finish what he has started; partly because he could not bear to face his comrades afterwards. His decision is helped by the cries of Langon, and hardened by the abuse of Bessie. In the end he 'roughly releases her grip, and pushes her away from him', in spite of her anguished appeal: 'Don't fling me from you, now!' Nora is left, weakly calling after him; Bessie, who a minute previously had been a mocking fury, comes to Nora, lifts her, and carries her into the house, realizing that Nora is about to give birth. Fluther enters roaring drunk, and is dragged into the house by Bessie, who would like to send him for a doctor. After Mrs Gogan has refused to go, Bessie walks out, fortifying herself with a prayer.

fanlight A (usually) fan-shaped small window over a door.

area i.e. a small sunken court, giving access to the basement of a building.

I wouldn't put much pass on that I wouldn't pay too much heed to it. (See how Mrs Gogan minimizes the true sufferings of her daughter.)
folly Follow.
in dhread any minute Another longing vision of death; notice how she follows it by a reassuring question of Mollser.
up the town Towards the centre of Dublin.
Nelson's Pillar It stood much shorter than the column in London's Trafalgar Square, opposite the GPO building. It was blown up in the 1960s.
The Parnell Statue This stood in the same street.
we seen th' Lancers See the section on 'Background'.
blighters Polite slang for 'ruffians'.
The gunboat *Helga* ... Liberty Hall See section on 'Background'.
shanghaied i.e. in trouble.
th' boyo hasn't a sword on his thigh now. A reference to The Minstrel Boy – the brave young hero of the poem of that name in Moore's *Irish Melodies*. This is a scathing reference to the rebels of 1916.
oul' Orange bitch Protestant Ulsterwoman.
a wild card i.e. a wild lively character.
dhressed in th' habit of Saint Francis A Franciscan Friar's robe. Another fantasy, beautifully expressed in Mrs Gogan's best (unwittingly comic) tragic manner.
th' wicked are at rest A parody and reversal of the hymn line.
tossed Dishevelled.
risked more for love ... risk for hate She knows she went into terrible danger alone and unarmed: the women who reviled her stood with their armed comrades behind a barricade. This is the first of a number of speeches by Nora about courage and cowardice.
He is to be butchered She unconsciously echoes the words of the speaker at the meeting: the dead are earlier rebels who were killed.
Sorra mend th' lasses Roughly, 'They asked for trouble and now it's come to them.' Bessie too has little time for women who encourage their men to be heroes.
Stabbin' in th' back Bessie is a fervent loyalist: she believes that Ireland stands or falls with the rest of Great Britain – and she remembers her own son in the army.
jilt i.e. trifle with.
judgements are prepared Again the hint of the scriptures.
a power o' Many.
I can't help thinkin' every shot Nora feels, more strongly than her husband, the bond that should unite them.

hussy Woman who behaves in a bold 'unwomanly' way.
I wasn't worthy to bear a son We have our second hint that Nora is with child, and further evidence that she puts her marriage vows before all else.
they're afraid to show they're afraid She will develop this theme later – and there is a good deal of truth in it. The feeling is known to most people who are doing dangerous work.
Th' agony I'm in A touching speech, full of faith and love.
only for Fluther If Fluther hadn't helped.
th' tossers The coins and wooden strip used in 'two-up'.
You an' your leadhers She underlines the difficulties of getting about the streets for food, and mocks the men for being afraid.
A lot o' vipers Ungrateful people; but ironical, in that St Patrick is said to have driven poisonous snakes from Ireland.
an' keep us from th' sin o' idleness Gambling, to him, counts as work.
oul' son A rough endearment.
turn-up Affair.
a juice A deuce – twopence ('tuppence').
Harps The sign on the obverse ('tail' side) of an Irish penny.
tanner Sixpence.
off to heaven in a fiery chariot Like the prophet Elijah, 2 Kings, 2.
th' Volunteers is firin' on them In their determination and crusading zeal they are prepared to destroy the people they are supposed to be helping.
she'd dhrop every minute She would die of a heart attack.
Th' selfishness of that one He was showing a good deal of selfishness himself.
tiltin' at me an' crossing me Jeering and thwarting me.
Wrathmines Rathmines, a fashionable 19th-century suburb of Dublin.
I have to go away, ma'am A euphemism for 'looting'.
game Lame.
Dunboyne Ten miles or so from Dublin.
jamb Upright part of door frame.
runnin' hurry of an inthrest Your sudden interest.
puttin' aside th' harp . . . unicorn. You may be interested in these symbols of old Erin, but I'm interested in the symbols of a royal Britain.
a fat wondher A great surprise.
sky-thinkin' Thoughts of heaven.
pinch anything dhriven asthray Steal anything left lying about. (But the two women unite when Peter wants to join them.)
live with from backside to breakfast time A coarse way of saying 'knowing well and intimately'.

a Christian kinch Christianity has always had a tight hold on her conscience.

sorra mind I'd mind I would not mind at all.

met with a dhrop Were injured or killed.

endeyvours Efforts.

ketch Snap up.

a cross off an ass's back There is a cross-shaped mark on a donkey's back. If everyone were blind, says The Covey, Peter would try to steal even that – an impossible task.

long, lanky lath Tall thin strip.

the pride of a great joy Another Biblical echo.

stitched a sthray ... shame out o' them When we've raised the necklines to a respectable height, so that we shan't look like loose women.

cuban heels Low by our contemporary standards, but high then.

Why did you fire over their heads? The following lines tell of how the mob turned on the rebels.

knocking around To be found.

The minstrel boys ... out of their hands Another reference to Moore's famous song.

choke the chicken i.e. she is twitting him about his occupation.

I must go, Nora Clitheroe doesn't want to break faith with his comrades: she doesn't want him to break faith with her.

What possessed you He shows his fear of what his comrades would think.

No more, maybe That doesn't matter – he means everything to her.

renegade Deserter, traitor even.

look, Jack She returns to the theme of the fear of fear.

a new tunic-shirt One buttoning all the way down the front.

I'll thrim your thricks I'll stop your drunken dancing.

Act 4

The room is one of the poorer ones in the house occupied by the Clitheroes. It is described in great detail, and is seen to be much less clean and tidy. The two patches of colour come from the looted articles; the evidences of the rebellion are the bullet-scarred window – grim forecast of what is to come – and the light from burning houses.

Peter and The Covey have been playing cards by the light of candles placed on a coffin, which we soon learn holds the corpses of Mollser and Nora's baby – prematurely born and, one supposes, soon dead, if not dead at birth. There is no particular significance in this gaming in the presence of death – it is almost in the tradition of the wake. Fluther is peeping out of the window, and is urged by the others to come away. They have had experience of shots being fired at their window – by troops who had been sniped at by rebels from the buildings. Fluther joins in the game, while a moan from Nora is heard from the other room, and a voice in a distant street is heard calling for an ambulance.

As the conversation continues, we learn that Nora is demented, thinking only of her husband and her child, and that Bessie has exhausted herself in looking after her; we remember how she went out (at the end of Act 3), at great personal risk, to fetch the doctor. For the first time the men say something good of Bessie; but they break off to quarrel over the game, thus waking her and bringing her in to quieten them. She is exhausted, and tells of her struggle to calm the unfortunate Nora, who has the 'idea that dead things are livin' an' livin' things are dead'.

Brennan now enters. Like so many Volunteers and Citizen Army men he has cast off his uniform and is wearing a suit. He brings the news that Clitheroe is dead, killed in the collapse of the defence at the Imperial Hotel. There is irony in the words 'Comrade Clitheroe's end was a gleam of glory' (the hotel was in flames); again in the idea that Nora's grief will turn to joy when she realizes that she had a hero for a husband (she wanted a living husband, not a brave rebel, as we saw in Act 1). (We are also aware of irony when we remember Clitheroe's toast in Act 2: 'Death for th' Independence of Ireland'.)

Nora now enters, confused. She is reliving past country rambles with Jack; then breaks off to recall their last meeting and parting (Act 3). After this she screams for her baby and her husband, and is quietened by Bessie who promises to sing to her, and leads her away singing 'Lead, kindly light', a true underlining of the way Bessie has been supporting the weak. This hymn-singing is absolutely in Bessie's strong Protestant tradition.

When Brennan – understandably scared – says he stands no chance in the streets, and must stay, Peter and The Covey run true to form and show alarm. Fluther takes control, giving a hint of the courage he showed when he went looking for Nora. Almost immediately, Corporal Stoddart comes in. Speaking in O'Casey's usual appalling travesty of an English accent, he orders the men to carry out the coffin. He asks the cause of Mollser's death, giving The Covey a chance to give a little lecture on Socialism. The four men and Mrs Gogan go out with the coffin – after Mrs Gogan has referred to Bessie's kindness to Mollser.

Stoddart, who has already talked about rebel snipers, says that all men in the district have to be rounded up because some have given aid to the snipers. He expresses the belief that all able-bodied Irishmen should be conscripted, but assumes that those in the room are Sinn Fein supporters. He is answered by a tirade from Bessie, during which she reveals that her son – one of the first to join the Dublin Fusiliers at the outbreak of the Great War – has been severely wounded and is on his way home.

When the four men return, Brennan, not wishing to attract attention, slinks into a corner, while the rest plunge into one of their frequent quarrels, after which they prepare to start another game. They are told by the Corporal, however, that they must go with the other men of the district to temporary detention in a Protestant church. [This is taken from O'Casey's own experiences in the Easter Rising.]

There is the sound of a shot and a scream of pain, and Sergeant Tinley enters with the news that one of his men has been hit by a soft-nosed bullet; he rather foolishly expects the rebels to come into the open and fight fair – hardly a sensible tactic in street fighting! Fluther, having exaggerated the number of troops involved, is forced from the room. After the men have left, Nora enters: thinking she is in her own home, she fills a kettle to make tea. She lays the table, sings her favourite song (and Jack's). Suddenly she calls for her baby and her husband, and rushes for the window. Soldiers shout to her to get away from it, and an awakened Bessie tries to drag her off, but in the struggle Bessie is herself thrown against the window and is shot.

As she lies dying, her speech becomes a combination of vituperation and pleas for help; but Nora, the woman whose life she has saved, thinks only of a dead man. Bessie dies, her only consolation being the hymn she struggles to finish. Mrs Gogan enters, and is talking about the 'poor inoffensive woman' (it has taken Bessie's death to bring forth this quite false estimate of her character) when the Sergeant and the Corporal rush in. They are shaken by Bessie's death, but say that they could not afford to take any chances. Nora screams, and begs Mrs Gogan to cover up the body. Mrs Gogan does so, typically revelling in the description of the dead woman, then leads Nora away, to the dead Mollser's bed – again typical, we feel. She relishes the thought of laying Bessie out. Seeing the kettle boiling, the soldiers make tea and, as the general attack on the Post Office begins, they sing [with perhaps conscious irony on the part of O'Casey], 'Keep the home fires burning'.

wash-stand With holes in the top for jug and basin.
playing cards ... coffin It was quite a common thing for people to keep the corpse company and amuse themselves while doing so.
The sky's gettin' reddher and reddher The troops were carrying out the commander's policy of burning the rebels out.
you'll only bring a nose on th' house You'll have someone suspecting you of being a sniper.
pimpin' He really means 'peeping out'.
Spuds Spades.
Thray Three.
snuffed it Died.
How could she The first of the references The Covey makes to tuberculosis; (see section on 'Background').
th' chloroform she got To ease the birth-pangs and relax her muscles.
hand runnin' Consecutive.
gut yous Rip you both open.
spread that out i.e. make it last.
whipped away Captured or killed.
she'll never be much betther A vivid description of a half-demented woman.
civvies An ordinary suit.
th' Imperial Hotel The ICA made its last stand here. Ironic that it should belong to the man who caused them to strike and then locked them out.
leppin' spout A leaping column.
our General General Connolly.
you're going away ... can't follow you Just as he has been behaving all through the play.

Lead, kindly light There is nothing unusual in Bessie's singing this hymn: she is a Protestant one of the sort to whom hymns, prayers and the scriptures come as naturally as breathing.

trench tool Short-handled, small-bladed implement for digging fox-holes for temporary cover.

is that all? The Covey's second reference to consumption [something only too familiar to O'Casey].

cheese it Stop it.

dawg-foight To one who had been in a big battle, the rising was simply a dog-fight – a difficult and bloody one, however.

give 'im the cold steel Bayonet him. Snipers were not popular on any front.

I'll never forget what you done Another reference to Fluther's courage.

It's meself that has well chronicled Here Mrs Gogan refers to Bessie's unpublicized kindnesses.

I'd make 'em all join hup A reference to the conscription being introduced in England, which had never applied to the Irish, though great numbers of them volunteered.

Shinners Sinn Fein sympathizers.

harness herself for Church Put on her best clothes.

whose only son went to th' front We hear of his return, wounded.

a hot shop i.e. very dangerous.

lowsers Lousy brutes.

hearse-man Coffin bearer.

bowseys Drunkards.

th' Man above God.

sliddherin' Slippery.

picaroons Rogues.

you'll be gowing out of 'ere i.e. to be interned, temporarily, in a church. [A reference to O'Casey's own experience.]

I do loike I do like a nice mince pie – from a music-hall song of the time.

Dum-dum bullets The bullet has no nickel coating; the result is shown by the Sergeant's words. It was a detestable missile, banned by the Geneva Convention.

Hassassins i.e. assassins.

foight fair A touching hope. Fluther is right when he points out how ridiculous the idea is.

press Cupboard.

Th' violets Nora reverts to her favourite song, with its associations with Jack and their young love.

Jack! ... my baby! The action that follows has been forecast at the beginning of the scene.

a look of agonized astonishment One of the classic reactions to being wounded.

Nora, hold me hand Remember how she had soothed Nora earlier.

I do believe Not just a theatrical trick; the singing of a hymn to comfort her last minutes is absolutely in character for one of her background.

th' poor inoffensive woman Now Mrs Gogan's views have changed.

couldn't afford to toike any chawnces To the soldier, clearly visible in the open, any movement at a window, which might be a sniper's loophole, was a danger.

Her face has written on it Mrs Gogan's favourite theme again.

scald Tea.

They were summoned Verse of a popular World War I song composed by Ivor Novello.

There's a silver loining There must be some ray of hope for the ordinary soldiers and civilians.

the boys come owme By ending the play with this British soldiers' song, O'Casey is really referring to Bessie Burgess's son and the other 400,000 Irishmen who enlisted voluntarily. And O'Casey knew the struggles they were to face after the war.

General revision questions

1 Write a character sketch of the most interesting person in *The Shadow of a Gunman*, indicating clearly his/her contribution to the action of the play.

2 In what ways is O'Casey a 'compassionate' writer? You may refer to one or both of the plays in your answer.

3 How does O'Casey create a particular atmosphere in either of the two plays?

4 Write a character sketch of Nora, indicating how she influences the course of the action in *The Plough and the Stars*.

5 Write an essay on O'Casey's humour in either or both of the plays.

6 In what ways is a study of the background helpful in considering these plays?

7 Write a character sketch of either Davoren or Clitheroe.

8 Consider the part played in his respective play by either Seumas or Fluther.

9 In what ways does O'Casey show development of character in either or both plays?

10 Write an essay on the nature of the language *either* in one play *or* in both.

11 What is the message underlying either *The Shadow of a Gunman* or *The Plough and the Stars*?

12 In what ways is O'Casey non-political? You should refer to one or both of the plays in your answer.

13 Write an essay on O'Casey's presentation of English speech, particularly in *The Plough and the Stars*.

14 In what ways is either play a tragi-comedy? Refer closely to the text in your answer.

15 Consider the roles played by the main female characters in either of the plays.

16 Write an essay on O'Casey's use of contrast in either of the plays.

17 How does O'Casey succeed in maintaining dramatic tension in his plays?

18 Compare and contrast *The Shadow of a Gunman* with *The Plough and the Stars*. Which do you consider the more effective dramatically?

19 Write an essay on O'Casey's use of song in either or both of the plays.

20 'He takes no side; he merely reveals.' How far is tnis true of O'Casey's art in either or both of the plays?

Pan study aids Titles published in the Brodie's Notes series

W. H. Auden Selected Poetry
Jane Austen Emma Mansfield Park Northanger Abbey Persuasion Pride and Prejudice
Anthologies of Poetry Ten Twentieth Century Poets The Poet's Tale
Samuel Beckett Waiting for Godot
Arnold Bennett The Old Wives' Tale
William Blake Songs of Innocence and Experience
Robert Bolt A Man for All Seasons
Harold Brighouse Hobson's Choice
Charlotte Brontë Jane Eyre
Emily Brontë Wuthering Heights
Robert Browning Selected Poetry
John Bunyan The Pilgrim's Progress
Geoffrey Chaucer (parallel texts) The Franklin's Tale The Knight's Tale The Miller's Tale The Nun's Priest's Tale The Pardoner's Tale Prologue to the Canterbury Tales The Wife of Bath's Tale
Richard Church Over the Bridge
John Clare Selected Poetry and Prose
S. T. Coleridge Selected Poetry and Prose
William Congreve The Way of the World
Joseph Conrad The Nigger of the Narcissus & Youth The Secret Agent
Charles Dickens Bleak House David Copperfield Dombey and Son Great Expectations Hard Times Little Dorrit Oliver Twist Our Mutual Friend A Tale of Two Cities
Gerald Durrell My Family and Other Animals
George Eliot Middlemarch The Mill on the Floss Silas Marner
T. S. Eliot Murder in the Cathedral
Henry Fielding Joseph Andrews
F. Scott Fitzgerald The Great Gatsby
E. M. Forster Howards End A Passage to India Where Angels Fear to Tread
William Golding Lord of the Flies The Spire
Oliver Goldsmith Two Plays of Goldsmith: She Stoops to Conquer; The Good Natured Man
Graham Greene Brighton Rock The Power and the Glory
Thom Gunn and Ted Hughes Selected Poems

Thomas Hardy Chosen Poems of Thomas Hardy
Far from the Madding Crowd Jude the Obscure The Mayor of Casterbridge
Return of the Native Tess of the d'Urbervilles The Trumpet-Major

L. P. Hartley The Go-Between The Shrimp and the Anemone

Joseph Heller Catch-22

Ernest Hemingway For Whom the Bell Tolls The Old Man and the Sea

Barry Hines A Kestrel for a Knave

Gerard Manley Hopkins Poetry and Prose of Gerard Manley Hopkins

Aldous Huxley Brave New World

Henry James Washington Square

Ben Jonson The Alchemist Volpone

James Joyce A Portrait of the Artist as a Young Man

John Keats Selected Poems and Letters of John Keats

Ken Kesey One Flew over the Cuckoo's Nest

Rudyard Kipling Kim

D. H. Lawrence The Rainbow Selected Tales Sons and Lovers

Harper Lee To Kill a Mockingbird

Laurie Lee As I Walked out One Midsummer Morning Cider with Rosie

Thomas Mann Death in Venice & Tonio Kröger

Christopher Marlowe Dr Faustus

W. Somerset Maugham Of Human Bondage

Arthur Miller The Crucible Death of a Salesman

John Milton A Choice of Milton's Verse Comus and Samson Agonistes
Paradise Lost I, II

Sean O'Casey Juno and the Paycock Shadow of a Gunman &
The Plough and the Stars

George Orwell Animal Farm 1984

John Osborne Luther

Alexander Pope Selected Poetry

Peter Shaffer The Royal Hunt of the Sun

William Shakespeare Antony and Cleopatra As You Like It Coriolanus
Hamlet Henry IV (Part I) Henry IV (Part II) Henry V Julius Caesar
King Lear King Richard III Love's Labour's Lost Macbeth
Measure for Measure The Merchant of Venice A Midsummer Night's Dream
Much Ado about Nothing Othello Richard II Romeo and Juliet The Sonnets
The Taming of the Shrew The Tempest Twelfth Night The Winter's Tale

G. B. Shaw Androcles and the Lion Arms and the Man Caesar and Cleopatra
The Doctor's Dilemma Pygmalion Saint Joan

Richard Sheridan Plays of Sheridan: The Rivals; The Critic;
The School for Scandal

John Steinbeck The Grapes of Wrath Of Mice and Men & The Pearl

Tom Stoppard Rosencrantz and Guildenstern are Dead

J. M. Synge The Playboy of the Western World
Jonathan Swift Gulliver's Travels
Alfred Tennyson Selected Poetry
William Thackeray Vanity Fair
Flora Thompson Lark Rise to Candleford
Dylan Thomas Under Milk Wood
Anthony Trollope Barchester Towers
Mark Twain Huckleberry Finn
Keith Waterhouse Billy Liar
Evelyn Waugh Decline and Fall
H. G. Wells The History of Mr Polly
John Webster The White Devil
Oscar Wilde The Importance of Being Earnest
Virginia Woolf To the Lighthouse
William Wordsworth The Prelude (Books 1, 2) Wordsworth Selections
W. B. Yeats Selected Poetry

Australian titles

George Johnston My Brother Jack
Thomas Keneally The Chant of Jimmie Blacksmith
Ray Lawler Summer of the Seventeenth Doll
Henry Lawson The Bush Undertaker & Selected Short Stories
Ronald McKie The Mango Tree
Kenneth Slessor Selected Poems
Ralph Stow The Merry-Go-Round in the Sea To the Islands
Patrick White The Tree of Man
David Williamson The Removalists